Monday Magic

Tina Mistry

by the same author

GRAN'S DRAGON
HIGHDAYS AND HOLIDAYS

Monday Magic

MARGARET JOY

illustrated by Rowena Allen

ff

faber and faber

*First published in 1982
by Faber and Faber Limited
3 Queen Square London WC1N 3AU
Printed in Great Britain by
Redwood Burn Ltd, Trowbridge, Wiltshire*

British Library Cataloguing in Publication Data
*Joy, Margaret
Monday magic.
I. Title
823'.914 [F] PZ7*

ISBN 0-571-11924-7

Contents

For all my friends in schools

CHAPTER ONE

Magic in Class

"JACK AND HIS mother were very poor and often had no food in the house at all," began Miss Jelly at story-time. Her class sat round her, listening wide-eyed. They shook their heads sadly.

"Canna goat the toilet?" asked Isabel plaintively. Miss Jelly nodded automatically and went on. Isabel clattered out.

"So Jack had to take the cow to market to sell her..."

"Why didn't they eat the meat off the cow?" asked Erica sensibly.

"Because the cow was their pet really," said Miss Jelly, "and they were very sorry to sell her. Then on the way to market Jack met a man who said he would buy the cow. He gave Jack some magic beans and Jack took them home to his mother."

"And they had beans on toast!" cried Gavin delightedly.

"Nah!" said red-haired Johnny scornfully. He had heard this story before. "She shot them out of the window and they growed in the night and..."

"Our beans din't grow in the night," said Pete, glancing at a row of jam-jars on the window-sill.

"Ours is in blotting-paper anyway."

"Ours isn't magic either; ours is just ornery beans."

Miss Jelly's class stared, disappointed, at the beans they had planted some days before. Isabel came in again noisily and sat down.

"There was a man on telly did some magic," suggested Desmond brightly. "He said magic words what rhymed – ".

"Like *bring and . . . thing!*"

"Or chalk, an' . . . talk!"

"*Old and gold!*"

"Posh and nosh!"

"Pale an' . . . ale!"

"School and rule!"

"Or *Jelly an' . . .*"

"Smelly!" suggested Desmond daringly. They nudged one another and giggled, looking sideways at Miss Jelly to see her reaction.

"Telly," she said firmly. "Telly and jelly."

"An' you gotta have a wand," went on Desmond, carried away by his own ideas.

"Miss Jelly han't gotta wand."

"She gotta ruler."

"But it's gotta be sparkly, like."

"Put a milk-bottle top on, get a milk-bottle top."

Miss Jelly decided to play along. "All right, we'll magic the beans!" She stuck the milk-bottle top on the end of her ruler with a blob of glue. "I'll wave my wand and say the magic words, and you must all help me. Are you ready?"

There was perfect silence as they waited for the spell to begin. Miss Jelly waved the wand slowly three times

over the beans and the class solemnly chanted the responses.

"*Bring –* "

"Thing!"

"*Chalk –* "

"Talk!"

"*Old –* "

"Gold!"

"*Posh –* "

"Nosh!"

"*Pale –* "

"Ale!"

"*School –* "

"Rule!"

"*Telly –* "

"JELLY."

The children waited expectantly. The beans in the jam-jars were still pressed lifelessly against the damp blotting-paper. The classroom was unusually still as the children held their breath. But the seconds passed and nothing seemed to have changed. The magic hadn't worked. Erica sighed.

"Ooh, look," said Charlotte in her piercing voice. "There's a great big spider on that jam-jar at the end."

Julie and Jean squealed and clutched each other with dramatic shudders. Other children scrambled to their feet.

Miss Jelly fetched the jam-jar at the end of the window-sill. They all leant forward excitedly to see the spider. There was a moment's disbelieving silence.

"'Tisn't a spider!" said Desmond. "It's too big."

"It's a sort of ball – ooh, look, it's moving!"

"It's jumping – where's it gone? There, look, on top of the blackboard!"

"It's blue, and green, and yellow, and purple, and – "

"It's like the rainbow!"

"It's all fuzzy an' furry!"

They were all crowding round the foot of the blackboard, gazing up at the fat round rainbow-striped ball. Miss Jelly's wand had slipped from her fingers and she leaned back on her table for support. She wiped her face with a paper tissue and bent over to check that the heating was off. Thank goodness it was nearly home-time. It had been a long Monday.

"Er ... children, that's enough," she said weakly, "Sit down now."

The fat little rainbow-striped wotsit stared down at them as if hardly able to believe his eyes. He was holding tight to the top of the blackboard with fat, furry, black arms. Suddenly he drummed noisily with his furry black feet. The children gaped and moved back.

"What *is* this?" he demanded in a high squeaky voice. "You lot never seen a Wotsit before? Siddown like she told you!"

The children obediently crumpled to the floor and sat scarcely breathing, staring at the plump little figure.

"She's telling you a good story there," he went on. "I wanta know what happens to them beans. Now pin back your ears and let me listen!" He turned his glittering black eyes on Miss Jelly, who had collapsed on to her chair.

"Right!" he ordered. "Now you've magicked me

here, we've all got to live together in this school, so there's got to be a spot of discipline! Now get on with the story and let's hear the end before the bell goes . . . !"

CHAPTER TWO

Mr Satterthwaite is Worried

FIRST THING NEXT morning it was register-time.

"Where's my red pen?" asked Miss Jelly.

"Is it on your table?" asked Rose, pushing her dark plaits back over her shoulders.

"Can I go and lend you one from next door?" offered Gavin.

"You can have a go of my felt tip," said Louisa, "only it's a green one."

"Got it!" said Miss Jelly, fishing in her drawer. "It was under the Batman masks," she added unthinkingly.

"Batman, Batma-a-an!" they started to chant in unison.

"That's quite enough!" said Miss Jelly, and shook her head at Isabel who was just going to make a request.

At that moment Mr Satterthwaite came bustling into the room.

"Good morning, Miss Jelly! Good morning, babies!"

"Good-morn-ing, Mis-ter-Satt-er-thwaite," they chanted docilely.

"A word in your ear, Miss Jelly." There was a

certain note in his voice which Miss Jelly had heard before. She looked at the floor. Isabel saw her chance. "Canna goat the toilet?" she demanded, pulling urgently at Miss Jelly's skirt. Miss Jelly nodded, her eyes still cast down.

"Just before home-time yesterday, Miss Jelly, I believe there was a certain ... disturbance in your classroom? I could hear noisy chanting from my room. It's very difficult to concentrate when classes get unruly ..." Miss Jelly had good reason to suspect that Mr Satterthwaite had been wanting to concentrate on the Australian Test Match commentary, but she wisely said nothing. He went on: "I know that when *I* started teaching – "

"When they still wrote in copperplate," thought Miss Jelly disrespectfully.

"Children were expected to sit and work in silence," went on Mr Satterthwaite reprovingly. "But these days ..." He looked at Miss Jelly.

"Isabel's bunged up the washbasin with a paper towel and it's overflowing!" reported Trixie triumphantly. From where she was sitting she could see the washing area.

Mr Satterthwaite moved hastily towards the door. "One more thing, Miss Jelly, before I go: the governors meet again later this morning, as you know. It's almost certain that as the numbers in school are dropping so fast – as we've discussed before – they are bound to give in to the Local Authority and make the decision to close the school by the end of next year."

"Is there nothing we can do?" asked Miss Jelly anxiously, as she moved towards the washbasins.

He shook his head sadly. "No, Miss Jelly, I really don't think so. But I've got my thinking cap on..."

A large green- and yellow-checked cap appeared at a jaunty angle on his head. Mr Satterthwaite looked suddenly puzzled and hurried off down the corridor, still wearing his new headgear.

"Thinking cap, my foot!" exclaimed the Wotsit, suddenly appearing on the back of Miss Jelly's table. "He just needs a bit of Get-up-and-go!" His glowing stripes made him look like a fat little rainbow-coloured pin-cushion. The children cheered when they saw him again, pointing and nudging one another. The Wotsit took no notice of them. He went on:

"They gonna shut this school down? Over my dead body! I like it here – better than Board Schools, better than Dame Schools, better than American Schools of Business Studies. I've tried them all! I'll see they don't shut this place down – and you all gotta help, see?"

He glared at the children who were crowding round.

"Get back over there and get on with what she told you to do!" he ordered. Johnny didn't move. "Gebback!" shrieked the Wotsit fiercely, "or you'll feel my sting!" He pulled round his tail and waved it threateningly round his head like a lassoo. At the end of it gleamed a sharp-looking point. Johnny jumped backwards and the children moved away to their activities, keeping a watchful eye on the Wotsit, who had now leaped across to the sand tray.

Miss Jelly came back from mopping up the floor. Isabel sat down meekly to play with the plasticine. Julie and Jean were standing putting straws in the milk. Gavin and Tom were busy arranging model dinosaurs in the dolls' house. Johnny, who was concentrating on a pencil sharpener, had nearly reduced a whole wax crayon to a pile of curly shavings. The others were doing jigsaws, the older ones were writing.

"Please Mr Wotsit, can I play in the sand?" asked Rose, chewing the end of one of her plaits.

"Surely you can, polite little girl!" answered the Wotsit with a smile, leaping up on to the top of a frieze board. He put his furry black head to one side. "Now suppose you tell me why they're gonna close this school?" he demanded.

"There aren't enough children," said Rose, shovelling sand into a bucket. "People are moving away."

"Moving outa this nice place? I bet this is a real nice village, isn't it?" asked the Wotsit, his colours flashing.

"Lots of my friends have moved," said Rose sadly,

looking up at the Wotsit. "My dad says there's nowhere to work here."

"Nowhere to work?" exclaimed the Wotsit, as if unable to believe his ears. "We'll soon change that! I reckon your nice Miss Jelly magicked me just in time."

He took off and zoomed across the classroom just above the children's heads. "See ya, Jelly Babies!" he called in a piercing voice, and soared away down the corridor at top speed.

CHAPTER THREE

Preparations for a Meeting

THE WOTSIT FLEW straight along the corridor, past the other classroom and past Mr Satterthwaite's room. A radio cricket commentary at low volume was accompanied by the clinking of delicate china teacups: preparations were in hand for the governors' meeting. The main door of the school was propped open to let in a cool draught, so the Wotsit flew straight outside. The hot spring sunlight caught the glowing rainbow colours of his fat little body as he soared up to tree-top level. He cruised over the village, his glittering black eyes taking in every detail.

The tiny cream-washed school stood in the middle of the village next to the cricket field. Mr Satterthwaite considered it the ideal situation for a school. At the far side of the field stood the village pub, the Umpire's Arms. Nearby stood five or six little shops, the church of St Barnabas with its squat square tower and the churchyard surrounded by dark green yew trees. Behind the school was a small bumpy field, used as a playing-field by the pupils and known in the village as Golden Hills. Scattered round the village were groups of houses and farms built on their own land at a distance from the village centre. A shallow river edged by tall elms whispered along idly beyond the Golden Hills. The Wotsit glided forward, noting how everything he could see lay basking in the spring sunlight. No wonder people were moving away – the village was gradually falling asleep!

He suddenly found himself in the centre of a flock of starlings coming up from behind. "Don't you signal when you overtake?" he shrieked, flashing his rainbow colours at them. The cloud of startled starlings quickly dropped down into a copse and hid there twittering anxiously until he'd gone.

The Wotsit's eye was caught by two people walking slowly towards the school gate. A sleek blue sports car was pulling up with a crunch of gravel next to the school and a cyclist was just leaning his bike against the back of the cricket pavilion.

"Ah, the governors," thought the Wotsit. "I'd better have something to eat to keep my strength up before I see what's going on in there." He dived down to the open window of Miss Jelly's classroom and sat on the window-sill, watching. Everyone seemed busy, chatting contentedly.

Arthur and Tom were drawing soldiers. "I'm going to be a soldier when I grow up," said Tom.

"So'm I," said Arthur delightedly. "Shall I call for you?"

The Wotsit dropped quietly to the bottom of the blackboard and picked up a piece of yellow chalk for his lunch. Munching greedily, he flew off unnoticed into the sunshine.

Five minutes later he felt very much fitter and looked very much fatter. He glanced at his reflection in a window – yes, he was a fine figure of a Wotsit. A fighting fit Wotsit! And now for the governors!

He zoomed round the outside of the school to Mr Satterthwaite's open window and settled himself behind the curtain. He was just able to see the inside of the room through a crack.

The headmaster was sitting in his usual place behind his table in the canvas chair with UMPIRE printed across the back. It was the chair he usually packed in his car to take to cricket matches, and in which he was most at ease. As it was a warm day he had his favourite white pullover slung round his tanned neck and tied loosely in front by the sleeves.

The lady seated stiffly on his right obviously disapproved of his casual clothes. She looked very businesslike in a grey suit and white blouse. On her knee lay an open pad over which she held her silver pen ready to take notes.

"Do you mind if we smoke, Mrs Wagtail?" asked the headmaster, already taking from his desk drawer an old blackened pipe and a tin of tobacco.

"Oh, I suppose as the window's open...." she shrugged grudgingly.

"Good, good," beamed Mr Steel, who was seated opposite her. He had come straight from the office. He took a cigar from his top pocket, sniffed it and lit it immediately. Mrs Wagtail looked from one to the other and sat up even straighter and more primly.

"Like children with lollipops!" she thought to herself in disgust.

Across the table Mrs Battersby, mother of Rose in Miss Jelly's class, winked at her sympathetically. Mrs Wagtail blinked in astonishment and busied herself with her pad and silver pen. "MEETING" she wrote at the top of the page, and underlined it. She thought for a moment, then wrote: "At Little Elmford village school. Present were: Mr Satterthwaite, headmaster; Councillor Mrs Priscilla Wagtail; Mr Steel, businessman; Mrs Battersby, parent."

The door opened and a very tall thin man in a dark grey suit and white polo-neck sweater entered, stooping in the doorway to smile vaguely at everyone. He lowered himself into the fifth chair.

"So sorry I'm late. I was just asking Pamplemousse's advice about stewing my wife's kidneys in wine."

Mrs Wagtail pressed her lips together in disapproval. She wrote: "And the Reverend James Godber, vicar of St Barnadas (late as usual)."

The meeting had begun.

CHAPTER FOUR

Mrs Wagtail Sees Red

"LADIES AND GENTELEMN," began Mr Satterthwaite, "as you know, we've met this morning to discuss the future of our little school. 'Little' is the important word – the Local Education Authority thinks that we are too little, that we don't have enough children to make it worth keeping the school open. They say our children should go by bus each day to Potterton School, five miles away. I should like your opinions." He puffed hard at his pipe as the others sat silent.

The Reverend James Godber said: "This is a delightful village, and the school children are important members of our community. I think they should continue to be educated in our own school – which many of their parents and even grandparents attended – which is at the centre of our village life. Think how we should miss their little harvest festivals and Christmas plays and pantomimes, and Sports Day on the cricket field!"

Mrs Battersby beamed at him, nodding vigorously. "Quite right, vicar, quite right! It's lovely to look across the green and see our children at playtime and going for walks. And we can always call in and have a word with the teachers. My Barney is getting on well with Mrs Williams, and our Rose is so happy in Miss Jelly's class – I'd hate to pack her off on a five-mile bus ride every morning and not see her till four o'clock."

Mr Steel took his cigar from his mouth to speak, but Mrs Battersby turned to the headmaster and went on: "Do you know, Mr Satterthwaite, I even know what our Rose is having for dinner every day? If I just walk past the school kitchen windows about eleven in the morning, I can guess that it's liver and onions or chicken and stuffing, or curried eggs, just from the lovely smell!"

Mr Satterthwaite smiled. "Yes, indeed, it would be hard to beat our Monsieur Pamplemousse even in the best restaurants!"

Councillor Mrs Wagtail had heard enough. "Sentimental rubbish!" she cried. "This school has very few pupils, and they are growing fewer every year. The school is not economical to run. It would cost the ratepayer far less to bus the children to Potterton. The L.E.A. is almost certain to close the school in the very near future!"

"Shame!" said Mrs Battersby fiercely. The vicar shook his head very sadly. Mr Satterthwaite puffed automatically at his pipe and looked hard but unseeingly at the picture on his wall, "Sunset over The Oval".

Mr Steel coughed and said: "Of course if the Council did close the school it could always sell the buildings and the land. Sometimes, of course, the buildings themselves are worthless and they're simply bulldozed..."

"Bulldozed!" exclaimed Mr Satterthwaite and Mrs Battersby indignantly together.

"Yes, indeed," replied Mr Steel, "the land is probably worth more than the buildings. Perhaps some firm..."

"Yours perhaps, Mr Steel?" asked the vicar pointedly.

Aha, thought the Wotsit.

"Well, er ... possibly, possibly," admitted Mr Steel. "I won't deny that my firm is always interested in acquiring pieces of land for building..."

"Building what, Mr Steel?" asked the vicar.

"Houses, old chap, houses," said Mr Steel, as if it were obvious.

"And houses are lived in by people," persisted the vicar, "and people have..."

"Children!" said Mrs Battersby triumphantly.

"And then our numbers would go up again," said Mr Satterthwaite hopefully.

"But by then the school would have been bulldozed!" pointed out the vicar.

Mrs Wagtail flipped to the back of her pad. "As I have already written to Mr Satterthwaite, the L.E.A. considers that Little Elmford School should have at least twenty more children on the register to continue as a school."

"Well, listen to me, Mrs Prissy Wagtail," said Mrs Battersby, getting rather red in the face and stabbing forward in the air with her finger. "I think it's disgraceful to shut down a perfectly good school just for the sake of saving a bit of money. There are some things money can't buy, and a happy well-run school is one of them! I represent all the parents and we want the school kept open!"

Mrs Wagtail's cheeks turned very pink. She

consulted her notes once more. "I was hoping not to have to announce this yet, but I think perhaps the moment has come. The Council is prepared to give a last date: if the numbers of children attending this school have not gone up by twenty by the last day of June, the L.E.A. will close it down next year. That's really all I came to say," she finished in a dignified way. She picked up her pad and handbag and stood up, preparing to leave. The Wotsit thought this was the moment to leap out and confront the meeting, but something prevented him.

"Aaaagh!" screamed Mrs Wagtail.

The others shot up in their chairs. Mrs Wagtail was gazing in horror at the bottom of the door. A tide of red liquid was already seeping under it and into the room. Slowly, but definitely, the sinister-looking pool was moving towards Mrs Wagtail's smart shoes.

"Aaaagh! Blood!" she screamed again. There was no way out by that door. She leapt up on to her chair.

Mr Godber, Mr Steel and Mrs Battersby had moved quickly to stand like bodyguards round Mr Satterthwaite at the other side of his desk. They all stared with disbelieving eyes at the advancing tide. Suddenly there came a loud knocking at the door.

"Mr Satterthwaite? . . . Don't open your door just at the moment, will you?" came Miss Jelly's voice. "There's been a bit of an overflow again . . . Isabel . . . the bucket of red paint . . . but I'll have it cleaned up in five minutes . . . I think – please – just carry on with your meeting as though nothing had happened."

CHAPTER FIVE

Dinner Time at Little Elmford School

HALF AN HOUR later Mr Satterthwaite's room was empty, the curtains wafting gently out through the wide open window. The vicar had gallantly gone out first, squeezing his lanky body through the frame. Then he had helped a furious Mrs Wagtail to climb from the safety of her chair and through the window. She barely thanked him. "First a pointless meeting," she snapped, "then a horrifying flood on school property (I shall have to report that), and finally I ladder my tights doing contortions to escape!"

She drove away very fast in her low, streamlined blue car. The vicar meandered off on his bicycle, breathing deep breaths of sunny mid-day air.

In the headmaster's room Mr Steel and Mrs Battersby were sitting in the corner furthest from the flood, sipping generous glassfuls of Mr Satterthwaite's best sherry, kept for moments of crisis. The more they sipped, the wider Mr Steel's smile became and the more Mrs Battersby chuckled. "Oh dear, oh dear!" she said happily. "*What* a meeting to remember!"

"Yes, indeed!" laughed Mr Steel. "But all the same, Mrs Battersby," he went on, "I think the school's future does look very black. Every month one or two small schools are having to close down. I shall be very sorry to see it happen, of course. But if it does – "

"Your firm will try to make money out of it, eh?"

He shrugged. "I'm first and foremost a businessman, Mrs Battersby."

She put down her glass and stood up, ready to leave. "Well, we shan't give up without a fight – you'll see!"

Meanwhile the headmaster had rolled his trousers up to his knees and had stuffed his socks into his pocket. His shoes were tied together by the laces and were hanging round his neck. It reminded him of his boy scout days. He had paddled through the red flood to Mrs Williams's room, and she had led all the children out barefoot through the water.

"Remember Moses and the Red Sea," she called over her shoulder. Once outside the children ran about excitedly in the midday sun, feeling the warm grass like the promised land under their bare toes.

Indoors Miss Jelly, in a pair of wellington boots, and Mr Satterthwaite, barefoot, were frantically brushing and mopping huge red tidal waves down the stone-tiled passage and out into the yard. "Good thing we're not one of those new open plan schools, carpeted throughout," said Miss Jelly brightly, trying to be as cheerful as possible.

"Just keep that Isabel right away from all water in future," growled Mr Satterthwaite. His shoes banged on his chest every time he mopped at the water. He stopped and pulled impatiently at the shoe-laces cutting into the back of his neck. "And for goodness sake, how did all that red paint get mixed up in it?"

"We had a bucketful, stirred lovely and thick, ready to paint that Post Office frieze you suggested," said

Miss Jelly reproachfully. "Telephone kiosk, mail van, post box..." Her voice trailed off as she saw Mr Satterthwaite's expression.

"Mistair Sattertwit! Mistair Sattertwit!" came a despairing cry from the school kitchen. The headmaster groaned. "Oh, it's Pamplemousse! I'd forgotten the wretched *déjeuners*!" He looked down crossly at his red-stained feet. "Coming, Pamplemousse!"

He leaned his sopping mop against the wall and padded into the kitchen. Monsieur Pamplemousse stood in his white overall and chef's hat, stirring busily.

"It is ready, Mistair Sattertwit! All is ready! The soufflé, he is delicious, he is ready to eat. The green salad, she is dressed to perfection – now I mix the custard for dessert. But the children – where are they?" He looked through the hatch at the small dining-room, with its tables set for eight, each decorated with a tiny glass of crocuses.

Monsieur Pamplemousse suddenly stopped stirring and stared at the headmaster's red-stained feet. "You have been treading the grapes, Mistair Sattertwit? You prepare a little English wine? *Vin rouge* de Little Elmford perhaps?" He looked eagerly at the headmaster, then shrugged in disappointment and turned back to his custard.

"I go to fetch the children, yes?" asked Mr Satterthwaite, who found his chef's English catching. He padded outside, put two fingers in his mouth and blew an atom-splitting whistle. The children, who now had their footwear on again, lined up obediently in front of him.

"Today," he announced, "Monsieur Pamplemousse has prepared cheese soufflé with green salad in a light French dressing, accompanied by home-made granary bread, followed by chocolate pudding and custard." The children cheered and filed in hungrily. School dinner was always one of the day's highlights.

Mr Satterthwaite felt a hand pull on one of the shoes still dangling round his neck. "Canna goat the...."

"Isabel!" roared Mr Satterthwaite, frowning a terrible frown and stamping his red-stained bare feet at her. Isabel backed away open-mouthed and lowered herself into the nearest chair. Mr Satterthwaite *was* in a funny mood today.

CHAPTER SIX

The Wotsit Gets Things Moving

"SO WHAT THIS school needs is publicity, see?" said the Wotsit, zooming round Mr Satterthwaite's room extremely fast.

The headmaster felt as if he were in the middle of a speeded-up colour cartoon film. He shut his eyes for five seconds, then opened them again. No good – that fat, rainbow-striped ... thing ... was still circling the room dizzily, shouting instructions at the top of its high-pitched voice.

He hadn't really believed the children in Class I when they had told him about their visitor. "Magic? Rubbish!" he had said to them. "There's no such thing as magic! If only there were – then all our school's problems could be solved." But now he knew what they had been trying to describe to him. He could never have imagined such an obnoxious little creature as this.

"Please, *please* stop flying round," he begged. "A little refreshment, perhaps," he suggested desperately.

"Ah, well now," said the Wotsit, coming to rest inside the Inter-Village Schools Cricket Cup on top of the bookcase. "That's what I call old-fashioned courtesy. I just fancy a stick of orange for now, thank you. Chalk, that is. Anti-dust chalk, if possible."

"Certainly, certainly," said Mr Satterthwaite, going to the nearest stock cupboard and bringing back a large box of assorted colours. The Wotsit's black eyes bluged greedily. He reached in with his fat furry arm and pulled out a long stick of orange chalk. Snap, crunch, crack! The chalk had soon gone, leaving the Wotsit with a light powdering of orange round his mouth. He licked his lips with his green tongue.

"Now, as I was saying," he went on, peering over the edge of the silver cup, "what you lot need is publicity. And *I'm* the one to help you! I've spent years at Business Colleges, so I know what I'm talking about. No one can buy anything they ain't never heard of! Agreed? Agreed!"

"But schools aren't like that," protested Mr Satterthwaite, closing his eyes again.

"Why not?" shrieked the Wotsit. "Tell me why not! Haven't they got something good they want all those kids out there to enjoy? They have? – Right! – Then you gotta tell their parents all about it! And you gotta tell other people what lucky kids some people got – the ones that go to Little Elmford Village School."

His high voice rang round Mr Satterthwaite's room. The silver cup vibrated and wobbled on the polished shelf.

"But we haven't enough parents," protested Mr Satterthwaite feebly. "That's the trouble. We need more children in the school. We've only got until the last day . . ."

"Of June. Yeah, yeah, I heard all that. You gotta find twenty more children? Then you gotta go out and look for 'em!" He jabbed in the air with a plump black hand. "Right then – how about a Protest March? First you write a handout that gets delivered to every family within five miles of here. You never know, the publicity might well decide people to move to a house in Little Elmford."

"But there's no work for them . . ." sighed the headmaster.

"Yeah, that's more difficult," agreed the Wotsit. "Well then," he went on, "what you need is publicity in the papers to bring employers here with jobs. How about a . . . national bell-ringing contest in that church tower of yours?"

Mr Satterthwaite winced and held his throbbing head.

"Or that nice Miss Jelly goes in for Miss Great Britain?"

Mr Satterthwaite opened his eyes wide and said in shocked tones:

"*Not* the sort of publicity we hope for!"

"Or you get one of those Test Match things fixed for your cricket field?"

Mr Satterthwaite's face brightened at the thought. Then he shook his head wistfully: "I don't think they'd accept our invitation... Still, I do begin to see what you mean about publicity."

The Wotsit went on eagerly. "And you get that Mr Steel to build a few more of his dandy little houses, and when people come out of curiosity to see what's going on at Little Elmford they might just take a fancy to one of them."

"But we've only got until the end of June," said Mr Satterthwaite.

"All the more reason to start work now!" shrieked the Wotsit, leaping up and down inside the silver cup.

"I'll put my thinking cap on," promised Mr Satterthwaite.

An England cricket cap appeared on his head, tilted over his right eye. "That's odd," he frowned, feeling his head. "I'm sure I didn't mean to play cricket in school this morning."

The Wotsit screeched with laughter at his own joke-magic, rolling round and round inside the cup. It wobbled to and fro on the very edge of the polished bookcase. He held his sides, still squealing with laughter and slid round inside the cup again. It wobbled, hesitated on the edge, overbalanced and fell. "He-e-e-elp!" squealed the Wotsit, panic-stricken. He didn't at all like getting hurt.

Mr Satterthwaite caught the cup, with the Wotsit still inside, before it reached the floor. "A lovely catch, silly mid-off, by Satterthwaite," he murmured, putting the cup back on the bookcase. "But you're right. It *is* serious. We'll have to see what can be done, Mr Wotsit. This school *must* be kept open somehow. We can't just let it die!"

Later that evening Barney Battersby was eating an orange and studying the *Radio Times*. He always worked backwards from the children's page and the coloured pictures, then progressed more and more quickly to the front. He squashed a large segment of orange into his mouth. "Ooh, gloog!" he exclaimed.

"Barna*bas*!" protested his mother. "There'll be yellow stains all over that *Radio Times* and I only bought it today."

"But look!" said Barney, swallowing heavily and pointing to a tiny announcement at the foot of the letters page. "Look, Mum – see there, where the splashes are – just read it!"

His mother held the magazine away from her face and screwed up her eyes. She read aloud: "We are planning to run a School Cook of the Year Competition, with a Grand Final on 31st May, televised in the finalists' schools. If you know of a suitable competitor, please send in the form below as soon as possible."

Barney hung over the back of his mother's chair, excitedly breathing orange all over her. "How about

Pamp, Mum? He's a great cook – couldn't we get him to go in for it?"

"We-ell, I don't see why not, but it's really up to him. You'd better go round and try to talk him into it. But don't tell anyone else: Monsieur Pamplemousse himself must decide. Here, take this to show him."

She handed the *Radio Times* to her son, who dashed out to find his friend, Timpo, and get to work on the chef.

"I just hope poor Monsieur Pamplemousse isn't allergic to oranges," murmured Mrs Battersby to herself.

CHAPTER SEVEN

A Chance Meeting

BARNEY PLODDED ON, pushing back his thick fair hair. His face was already streaked with grey from the printer's ink on his fingers. He had delivered most of his bundle of blue leaflets already, but he still had a few left. He glanced once more at the short message, composed by his mother, the vicar and Mr Satterthwaite.

> Little Elmford School must not be
> closed down. It is part of our
> village life!
> Please sign the petition in the
> Village Hall and come with us to
> join the Protest March and Meeting
> at Chesterby on Saturday.
> Coaches leave the school at 9 a.m.
> (Protest first, do your weekend shopping later!)

Barney certainly didn't want the school to close, but sometimes he wished something would happen, something to put Little Elmford on the map, as Mrs Williams said.

"But it *is* on the map," said several children in her

class, pointing to the ordnance survey map on the classroom wall.

"Ah," said Mrs Williams, "but it has to be on everyone's map, the map in their head. So if you say you live in Little Elmford, they immediately answer: 'Oh, yes, I've heard of that – isn't that the village where . . .'"

"Where what?" asked Timpo.

"That's what no one knows," said Mrs Williams, smiling. "That's why Little Elmford isn't on the map – yet."

Barney climbed on his bike. He had left it leaning against the wall of the Umpire's Arms, and now he needed it to deliver the last few leaflets to houses outside the village. He glanced at the list the vicar had given him: three outlying farms, a couple of bungalows, Green Acres, Mr Steel's big house with the builder's yard behind, and lastly Hilltop, Mr Adam's house.

Barney groaned. Not right up there: a one-in-four hill! And he was already tired out. He pushed his sticky hair back again from his hot forehead.

"Come on, come on!" snapped a nagging voice in his right ear. He shot round, but the road was empty. Then he realized that the voice was coming from beside his head. He shut his left eye and squinted hard. A fat, furry ball, striped in gaudy colours, was sitting on his shoulder. "Come on!" snapped the Wotsit again. "Standing there isn't going to win you friends and influence people! You gotta be vibrant, dynamic, energetic! Wotsit-power is what you need. I'll show you. Get on your bike!" he ordered. "Now where to?"

"Hilltop – up that twisting lane, there." Barney pointed, swinging himself on to the saddle.

"Hold tight!" said the Wotsit. Barney held the handlebars and started to pedal, but found that he needed only to steer; the Wotsit was somehow propelling him faster than he'd ever gone up a narrow, twisting one-in-four hill before. He still wasn't used to the strange and exciting feeling of speed when he reached the top and was outside Hilltop, panting with exhilaration and surprise.

Mr Adam himself was already in his garden. He was sitting very still on a bench, admiring the view across the valley to Chesterby. With his bright red cardigan, green cords and white beard, he looked rather like a garden gnome. "Hello, Barney," he said. "It *is* a hard climb, isn't it? No wonder you're gasping for breath! Here – let me fill your water-bottle for you."

The old man unclipped Barney's empty water-bottle and disappeared with it behind the house. "Don't forget why you came!" hissed the Wotsit.

"Leave it to me!" Barney hissed back, and pulled a rather crumpled blue leaflet from his pocket. The old man returned and gave Barney his water-bottle, now heavy and very cold. "My best spring water, straight out from the rocks." He waved vaguely up at the hill behind the house. "'Adam's Ale', I call it," and he laughed gently at his own joke.

Barney lifted the lid of the bottle and let the water trickle down his dry throat. It was icy cold, sharp and yet sweet, with a slight fizz that bubbled pleasantly in his mouth. "Mmm, that's great," he said approvingly, wiping his mouth with the back of his hand. "Thanks very much – oh, and here's a leaflet for you about our school."

Mr Adam smoothed out the blue sheet of paper and held it well away from his eyes. He read it carefully. "Mmm – school in trouble, is it? Great pity, I used to go there, you know, long ago ... long before you were born. But we can't just let a living school die. There's part of me in that school – and part of you too, Barney. Perhaps I could help ... I'll put my thinking cap on." Before Barney could say anything, a green velvet embroidered smoking cap with a swinging tassel had appeared on the old man's head. Mr Adam frowned, slightly puzzled. "We ... I'll be off then," said Barney hastily and swung himself on to the saddle. He started to free-wheel down the other side of the hill.

"I'll be off too," screeched the Wotsit from the handlebars. "I'm just off down to school for some supper: yellow and purple tonight, I think. See ya, Barney!"

The hill was extremely steep and the bike was gathering speed fast, too fast. Round a bend, down a steep straight slope, round another bend, Barney was frantically trying to hold the brakes on, whizzing round another bend – two figures were standing right in the middle of the quiet road. Barney clamped on his brakes. CRASSHHH!! He had swerved to avoid them and the wheels had skidded in the gravel, missing the two figures, but throwing Barney violently forward on to the grassy verge.

The next thing he was conscious of was something icy cold dribbling soothingly over his thumping head. He heard a boy's voice say:

"He'll be pretty fed up about his front wheel."

"And his knee," said another voice, "but Dad can straighten it with his tools."

"It's horribly buckled," went on the first voice.

"But my hanky's stopped the bleeding," said the second. Barney felt very confused and struggled to remember what had happened. He opened his eyes and found himself propped against the grassy bank at the side of the road. His bike with a buckled front wheel lay on its side nearby and his knee was covered by a rather grubby pad of handkerchief. A boy of about nine was squatting by his side, holding the water-bottle and dabbing drops of Mr Adam's spring water on to Barney's face. As his eyes opened, the boy's face lit up. In his relief he took a long swig from the bottle. "Mmm, super! You've woken up. At last!

You skidded in the gravel and took a header into the grass."

"Good thing you did," said the older boy, who was bending over the bent bike, "or you'd have bowled us over like skittles. We hardly saw you coming, and we can't move that fast on skates." Barney looked at their feet. They were both wearing roller skates.

"It's boring skating on the flat road at Green Acres," explained the younger boy. "We wanted somewhere more exciting..." His voice trailed off.

"Do you live at Green Acres?" asked Barney curiously. "Are you the Steel boys?"

They nodded their dark heads. "I'm Richard," said the older one, "he's Graham."

"I'm Barney Battersby," said Barney. He watched as they unbuckled their skates. "My mother's a school governor, like your dad."

Richard nodded. "But they're going to close your school soon, aren't they? Dad says they're going to."

"Oh no, they're jolly well not!" said Barney fiercely. He fished in his pocket and pulled out a leaflet. "Read that!" he ordered. "We're going to protest. All the village is. We don't want to go to rotten old Potterton School. They can't play football for toffee *and* they have foul school dinners. I know they do, because my cousin goes there."

"Well, ours are yukky too," said Graham. "At Trafalgar Towers we have squashed fly slices and frogspawn with raspberry sauce and soyaburgers and –"

"Poor old you," said Barney. "*Our* school chef makes great meals. He might even be going in for that TV competition for school cooks; we've asked him to. He's French and he's called Monsieur Pamplemousse.

He used to be in the French Resistance – you should see the scars on his arms!"

"What's he doing in your school then?"

"Oh, he came to work at the Ritz Hotel in London. When he retired he decided to stay in England. So he started work in our school."

"How did he get his scars?" asked Graham eagerly.

"Well, he had to blow up a railway bridge near to Paris to stop the enemy's trainloads of troops and ammo getting through. He blew it up all right, but he wasn't quick enough getting away, and a piece of metal hurtled through the air and sliced through his arm to the bone."

"Then what happened?"

"Well, luckily he knew a medical student – " began Barney, then stopped. "I tell you what – why don't you come on our Protest March on Saturday?" He grinned up at the two brothers. "Then you could actually see him and talk to him."

"Gosh!"

"Could we really? P'raps Dad'll come too, even if he does think the school will close. After all, he *is* a governor."

Barney struggled to his feet and they hauled him upright. "You O.K.?" He nodded, then grimaced at his buckled wheel. "We'll take it home," said Richard, "Dad'll straighten it in no time."

"Specially when we tell him it was our fault for being in the middle of the road."

"And we'll tell him about your chef and *make* him come on the March with us!" The Steel boys grinned at each other.

"Gosh!" said Graham again. "Do you think he'll let us see the scars . . . ?"

CHAPTER EIGHT

The Protest March

IT WAS A bustling, blue-skied Saturday morning. Most of the villagers of Little Elmford had managed to get to Chesterby early.

Shoppers in the town were amazed at the procession which slowly wound through the narrow streets. Two tractors led the way; noisy and slow, smelling of diesel, they chugged along, driven by the two Worton brothers.

Next came a horse pulling a cart full of the smallest children from the school. They were followed by ranks of parents pushing prams and pushchairs. The children had all brought musical instruments and were banging drums, shaking home-made maracas or making buzzing comb-and-paper music. The noise was indescribable.

Behind came the infantry – all the rest of the children of the school, marching along, accompanied by Mrs Williams, Mr Satterthwaite and Miss Jelly. Some of the children had made their own placards and banners, which they held up as they walked: "Little Elmford needs its own village school!" "Leave our school alone!" "Hands off our school!" and "Little Elmford School rules, O.K.!"

Monsieur Pamplemousse was there, too, in his chef's hat and white overalls. He was carrying a very artistic banner he had made himself in the shape of a frying pan. One side proclaimed modestly: "The best education and the best cuisine at Little Elmford School!" On the other side was written: "A good school works on its stomach!"

The two Steel boys had managed to work their way to Monsieur Pamplemousse's side and were eagerly asking him questions about his wartime experiences.

Timpo and Barney were nearly last in the procession, just behind the vicar and Mr Steel. Barney had ridden to Chesterby through the early morning on his perfectly repaired bike, and was now guiding it along beside him. Timpo had brought his pet rooster, Cocky Locky, and was carrying him under one arm. Every now and then Cocky Locky would crow loudly and add to the uproar.

The musical children and their parents at the front were now starting to sing new words to the tune of "John Brown's Body". The last line was aimed at any town councillors who might be listening:

"Little Elmford Scho-ol mu-ust never ever close,
Little Elmford Scho-ol mu-ust never ever close,
Little Elmford Scho-ol mu-ust never ever close,
Or we'll never ever vote for you again."

Next followed the music of "Polly Put the Kettle On". The words went:

"We don't want our school to close,

We don't want our school to close,
We don't want our school to close,
We like it where we are."

The children cheered, banging and shaking their instruments; Monsieur Pamplemousse waved his frying pan regally and Cocky Locky crowed raucously at the back of the procession. Isabel pulled at her mother's hand and whispered something. Her mother gave her a shake and dragged her onward.

PC 82 of the Chestershire Constabulary was on duty alone in the town centre. When he heard and then saw the cheering, singing procession led by two tractors, approaching, he immediately radioed HQ for reinforcements, which arrived on their bicycles: PC83 and Policewoman Crisp. As the procession seemed to be proceeding in an orderly (if noisy) fashion, the two policemen stood at each side of the road and watched the show. Policewoman Crisp smiled at all the children, waved to her nephew Gavin who was carrying a placard, and found herself tapping a neat black shoe in time to the chanting.

At the end of the singing there was much cheering and waving of placards. "Phew!" said Mr Steel. "This protesting is quite hot work." He wiped his forehead with a dark blue handkerchief. Barney had liked Mr Steel from the moment he delivered the repaired bike to the Battersbys' door. They found they both enjoyed tinkering with bikes.

"You can have a drink if you like," said Barney, pulling the cap off his water-bottle, and offering it to Mr Steel.

"Well, I don't mind if I do," admitted Mr Steel. "It

really *is* a warm morning for this time of year." He tipped up the bottle and drank a few mouthfuls. "Mmm," he said, "that was good. Most refreshing! Some sort of lemonade, was it?"

"Adam's Ale," said Barney.

"Oh?" said the vicar. "Could I try some?"

Barney carefully wiped the top of the bottle on his pullover and let the vicar have a swig. "Delicious!" agreed the vicar. "Reminds me of spring water I once drank in an underground grotto in the Alps: cool, sweet and bubbling – I've drunk nothing quite like it until now."

Barney told them where the water had come from and both the men looked surprised. "Didn't know there was a spring up on Norberry Hill," murmured the vicar, "and that reminds me, it's time I went to see Mr Adam again. It must be a lonely life up there on his own."

By now the bottle had been wiped again, this time on Timpo's pullover. It was his turn to drink, but whenever he tipped his head back, Cocky Locky tried to struggle free. Barney took Cocky Locky from him with his left arm, still trying to steer his bike with his right hand as he walked along. They had all reached the town centre and what seemed like most of the population of Little Elmford was now standing expectantly outside the massive Town Hall. Mrs Wagtail was spotted at an upstairs window, frowning at the noisy mob.

A dignified gentleman opened the door, received the signed petitions from the hands of Mrs Battersby and Mrs Williams, and promised smoothly that they would be seen by those whom they might concern.

"Three cheers for Little Elmford School!" shouted one of the Worton brothers, from the seat of his tractor. "Hip, hip, hurray!" shouted everyone enthusiastically. At that moment the excitement became too much for Cocky Locky, who pecked Barney's wrist. Barney automatically let go, grabbing his precious bike as it threatened to fall over. Cocky Locky flapped his great white wings madly, squawking at the top of his raucous voice, and landed on the Town Hall steps. The next minute he was making for the smooth gentleman who was holding the pile of petitions, and the smooth gentleman was moving faster than he had for months, streaking for the Town Hall door and slamming it shut in Cocky Locky's furious face.

Under cover of this little upset, Mr Satterthwaite turned to Miss Jelly. "Where's the Wotsit?" he asked in a low voice, out of the left corner of his mouth.

She answered in a similar low voice from the right corner of her mouth: "Locked in my stock cupboard. I saw him go in there last night when I was tidying up my classroom. I knew he'd come to no harm – there's plenty of ventilation – so I thought he'd be better out of the way today."

"You're probably right," agreed Mr Satterthwaite. "You realize he lives on chalk? He'll be fat as a barrel when you let him out on Monday morning." Miss Jelly nodded.

"Odd little creature, isn't he?" commented Mr Satterthwaite. "Irritates me a little, I'm afraid: rather like an overgrown schoolboy. Where did he come from, anyway?" he asked, looking over his shoulder just in case the Wotsit had escaped and was zooming around even now seeking a dreadful schoolboy revenge.

"We magicked him," said Miss Jelly. "A Class 1 spell."

"Oh," said Mr Satterthwaite thoughtfully. They marched on. "How long is he staying?" he asked casually.

"He says he likes it in our school."

"Oh," said Mr Satterthwaite very thoughtfully indeed. Then an idea occurred to him. "Don't spells work backward if you say them backward? That might do it." He said in a rather formal tone: "Perhaps you would kindly put your ... er ... spell in writing, Miss Jelly, and let me have it on Monday morning, nine o'clock sharp?"

Miss Jelly looked surprised.

"Well, yes, Mr Satterthwaite ... sir," she answered.

After the petitions were handed in, the Little Elmford protesters gradually dispersed, well pleased with themselves. However, the unusual Saturday morning commotion had already caused certain persons in the Town Hall to be even less well disposed towards the school than before.

CHAPTER NINE

Rose's Den

THE FOLLOWING MORNING Rose, Timpo and Barney went playing on the Golden Hills. There was nothing golden about them at present, as it was too early in the year for the brilliant yellow patches of broom and gorse which usually lit up the mounds in early summer. This Sunday there had been a sudden change in the weather; there were grey clouds rolling overhead, and a cold wind was blowing, which whistled in the children's ears and clawed at their coats.

Barney and Timpo were playing a sort of police game which they were making up as they went along. They had both brought model cars in their pockets and they had made for a big clump of broom with bare soil beneath it. With sticks and pebbles they were able to make motorways and race tracks. Soon the daring robbery and police chase was on.

Rose got bored watching. She had her teddy-bear Red Ted with her, so she held him tight to her chest and they ran up and down the hills for a little while, being Olympic skiers. Then they hid behind one of the largest grass-covered mounds and spied on the two boys. Rose called "Oy!", then ducked down so they couldn't see her. But after being startled the first time, the boys took no notice. Rose was bored.

"Wanna go home!" she called. The boys were sprawled full length on the grass under their bush, making little tracks in the dust. Again they took no notice.

Rose mooched away, still clutching Red Ted. On the side of a tiny hill in the corner of the field, a spot she had never really explored before, she found a place where some gorse bushes were growing in a horseshoe shape.

Rose went into the space inside the bushes and looked round. It was like a little room. And those stones at the end were like a fireplace. It was like one of Miss Jelly's stories – this was Cinderella's kitchen. Those boys were the horrid ugly sisters being unkind to Cinderella, who had to make a fire and do all the work.

Rose sat Red Ted at one side. "You're going to be my fairy godmother," she said. Then she set to work to clean up the fireplace. She brushed the hearth stones, then started to scrape out a hollow where she was going to put twigs and leaves to make the fire. It was hard work scraping, even though she had found a sharp stone to dig away at the soil with. Her hands were getting very dusty and they began to ache, the ends of her plaits kept getting in the way as she dug. She rubbed the back of her hands across her eyes. "I've got all this work to do and my ugly sisters have gone to the ball and left me," she sighed. She scraped a little more, and sighed again. "I wish I could go to the ball," she said, looking at Red Ted meaningfully. "But I've nothing to wear and . . ."

At this moment her scraping stone grated on something in the fireplace.

"Bother!" Rose forgot the patched rags she was dressed in, forgot her cold bare feet on the kitchen floor, forgot the prince's ball. She knelt down and scraped away some more soil, determined to clear a large flat square area for a hearth in her house.

Perhaps if she collected enough twigs and sticks they could have a real bonfire there. Perhaps her Mum and Dad would walk over and they could all come into her house. Perhaps her mother would bring some sausages to roast or bread to toast at the fire – in Rose's own kitchen fireplace! Her Mum often said people moved into a new house and had a house-warming – well, that really *would* be a house-warming, wouldn't it?

By now Rose had scraped away a great deal of the dirt. The object her sharp stone had grated on was sticking up above the ground. It seemed to be a kind of metal ring. It was fixed to something else, still stuck under the soil. She pulled, but it wouldn't move. What a nuisance! She *did* want to get her fireplace ready.

Her hands were getting cold in the chill wind, even though a pale sun had appeared in the sky. Rose went on poking and pushing and scraping away the soil from the metal object in the ground. Fairy godmother, Red Ted, sat propped uncomfortably against a gorse bush; his big brown eyes looked glassily into the distance and he smiled a knowing, fairy-godmother smile.

Rose was panting now, pulling and wiggling at the metal thing which was almost completely uncovered. She scraped hard a few more times and jogged again. The metal thing came out of its hole in the ground suddenly and Rose, who had been squatting, suddenly fell backwards. "Ooops!" she said and scrambled forward again on all fours to look at her find.

It was a round bowl with a handle on each side and a flat stand underneath. It reminded Rose of her mother's metal colander in which she drained the vegetables (only without the holes). It was also a little like the large china bowl, decorated with painted flowers, which her grandmother called a soup tureen. Rose was delighted. It was very dirty, but it was certainly a bowl – someone must have thrown it out. And now she had it for her kitchen. What a lovely den this was going to be! And it was *hers* – those boys hadn't found it. It was Rose's own secret – until she had her house-warming, that is, and invited people properly.

"Rose! Ro-ose!" called Barney's voice. They must be going home, and she didn't want them to go without her. Hastily she bent down and pushed the kitchen bowl as far under the gorse bush as she could without getting her face pricked.

She picked up Red Ted and hugged him tight. "It's going to be a lovely den, a *lovely* den!" she whispered. Then she started to run up and down over the grassy bumps and mounds towards Barney and Timpo.

CHAPTER TEN

An Odd Monday Morning

IT WAS MONDAY morning and Miss Jelly was taking in the dinner money.

"Desmond, why is it all in halfpence?"

"Cause me mam saves them in a whiskey bottle, and she hadn't got no other change."

"Gavin, where's your dinner money?"

"I put it in my sock so it would be safe, but I think it's slipped," said Gavin, limping across to her table with an anxious expression. He sat on the floor, took off his shoe and his sock and triumphantly shook the coins on to the floor.

"*I* brought mine in an envelope with my name on," said Julie self-righteously. Miss Jelly didn't answer. She had just hastily torn Julie's envelope across the top and torn the two pound notes inside in half. She was now busy with the sticky tape.

Next she counted the dinner money. It worked out correctly, thank goodness. She called the register. Everyone was at school except Johnny.

"Anyone know what's the matter with Johnny today?" she asked.

"He said to tell you he'd be sleeping in late this morning," volunteered Desmond.

"Yes, cause his mam's taking him to Chesterby to buy new shoes and have his hair cut," agreed Erica, who lived next door to Johnny.

"Oh," said Miss Jelly without comment.

She glanced across at the stock cupboard. There was still no sound from inside. She would have to open it soon. Surely he had been all right in there over the weekend?

At that moment Mr Satterthwaite walked in. There was an unusual spring in his step and a gleam in his eye. He was followed by a man, a woman in a scarlet dress carrying a baby, and three children. They all had shining black hair and deeply tanned skin.

"Good morning, Miss Jelly," beamed the headmaster. "May I introduce the Smith family? They have just er ... moved into the village."

Miss Jelly shook hands with Mr and Mrs Smith. She recognized the mother; she had been calling at the villagers' doors in the last week, carrying the baby under one arm and a large basket under the other, and selling pegs and bunches of chrysanthemums cleverly made of curled wisps of wood.

Miss Jelly had never taught gypsy children before. Mr Satterthwaite was going on: "Columbine and Eglantine, the twins, will be joining you, Miss Jelly, and Lupin is old enough to start in Mrs Williams's class." As he showed the parents and Lupin toward the door, he turned and hissed at Miss Jelly: "Three down – seventeen to play!"

She found the twins some building bricks and let them sit in a corner, where they could watch with their large brown eyes whatever was going on in the classroom.

"I'll just fetch a new packet of straws," said Miss Jelly casually, walking over to the cupboard. She unlocked the door very quietly and spotted the Wotsit lying snugly on his back in the now empty chalk box. The snuffly noises he was making reminded her of a baby in a carry-cot – surely he wasn't sucking his thumb? But something must have woken him, and the next minute he shot past her at waist-level. Like a heavily overloaded plane he seemed to be having difficulty getting airborne, and soon taxied down with a bump on the nearest table.

The children hadn't seen him for some days and crowded excitedly round. "Gerraway!" he yelped feebly, then groaned: "Ooow, my abdomen."

"What's the matter with the Wotsit? Miss Jelly, why's he making that funny noise? What's the matter with him?"

"His colours aren't so bright today," remarked Gavin.

"I don't think he's feeling quite so bright today," said Miss Jelly sympathetically. The Wotsit groaned heavily. She fetched the empty chalk box, lined it with some soft paper hankies, tipped it sideways and gently rolled him in. Rose fetched a doll's blanket from the Wendy House and laid it on the moaning Wotsit, whose eyes were now tightly closed.

Miss Jelly put the box carefully back on the shelf of the stock cupboard and shut the door. "Sssh," she said, her finger on her lips, "I think the Wotsit has a tummy-ache. Let's leave him alone for a while; he's eaten too much."

Isabel held her tummy in sympathy: "Canna goat....?" she began. Miss Jelly nodded and Isabel

hurried out. It was milk-time, and Erica's and Rose's turn to put in the straws.

As the children sipped or bubbled into their milk, the door opened again. It was a boy from Mrs Williams's class with a note, headed: Memo to Staff. Miss Jelly sighed. Mr Satterthwaite was *very* formal sometimes. It went on less formally: "I'm slipping over to the Council Offices in Chesterby to remind them that we're still here. And to tell them our numbers are going up (three more on roll today.) Humour Pamplemousse please – he's preparing steak and kidney pie with mushrooms followed by *crême caramel* – I don't want to risk a *scène de cuisine*. By the way, Miss J. – don't forget I want that spell in writing *today*.

W.G. SATTERTHWAITE

Monsieur Pamplemousse was alone in the school kitchen. His two "ladies", Di and Liz, had prepared the vegetables and other ingredients, and now they were in the dining room having their elevenses.

There was a sharp knock on the delivery door. He

wiped his hands on a damp cloth and went to open it. A young lady in denim jeans and jacket stood there, and behind her was a man in a sheepskin jacket. They both looked eagerly at the chef.

"Ah, you arrive?" he said, shaking each of them by the hand and ushering them into the kitchen. He quietly tiptoed across and shut the hatch. His dinner-ladies need not know – yet. "The headmaster, unfortunately he is gone out, but I'm sure he would not find your visit incommodious. I shall recount to him the whole story later. Mistair Sattertwit is a most reasonable man."

"So this is where it's all happening, is it?" asked the young man, looking round the neat kitchen with its rows of shining knives, polished pans and bunches of herbs hanging from the ceiling. His jaws chewed slowly as he gazed round with narrowed eyes, taking in all the details. "Right, Monsieur Pamplemousse," said the young lady briskly, pulling some papers from her shoulder-bag. "Now, let's talk business, shall we?"

CHAPTER ELEVEN

Something Old; Something New

Rose set out straight after tea. This time she had come prepared. She had a garden trowel, an old kitchen knife which would be useful for chipping the dirt off the bowl she had found, and a hearth brush. She ran across the cricket field, avoiding the clean-shaven grass of the wicket as Barney had taught her. Then she crossed the road and ran behind the school towards the grassy mounds.

"Yoohoo – Rose? Isn't that the polite little girl? Yoohoo!" Rose stopped and looked round. Pzzeeoinng! The Wotsit had shot towards her and landed feet first on her shoulder. His coloured stripes were gleaming and so were his eyes.

"Hello, Mr Wotsit," said Rose politely. "Are you better now?"

"Better? *Better*? I've never been ill, dear child! Never a day's illness in my life. Not even in the days when school started in the dark in the winter and oil lamps had to be lit, and there was no school milk, and all the children wrote on slates with slate pencils!"

"What did you eat if there was no chalk?"

"Oh, I managed on slate, but the chalk is much tastier and the selection of colours today is just fantastic. Do you know, they've brought out a new *luminous* chalk?... Ah, well, those were the bad old days, I suppose."

"But are you really better?" persisted Rose. "You weren't very well in Miss Jelly's cupboard!"

"Oh, that was nothing, nothing," said the Wotsit airily, "a slight indisposition. Just occasionally, one can be the tiniest, weeniest bit greedy... But now, let's forget that. You must tell me what's been happening while I've been ... recuperating."

"We've got two new ones in our class," said Rose eagerly. "Twin girls, Colly and Eggy we call them. Lupin's ten – he's in Mrs Williams's class. He knows all about birds and things. They live in that caravan behind the copse. They're gypsies."

"Three more children?" The Wotsit's eyes sparkled. "Splendid! Only seventeen to go! I seem to be having an effect on things already! And now, dear child – where are you off to?"

"Just over there," said Rose in an offhand way. "I'm making a den. You can come and look at it if you like."

"Lead the way!" cried the Wotsit, leaping off Rose's shoulder and hovering behind her until they reached the semicircle of gorse bushes. Rose went in. Nothing had changed. The fireplace stones were still arranged at one end, and there was quite a hole where she had finally managed to extract her kitchen bowl, like a resistant tooth, from the ground. She knelt beside the cavity. The Wotsit landed on the other side and they both peered in. The Wotsit looked up at Rose, puzzled.

"Nothing in there," he said.

"I'm just clearing out a wide space to make a fireplace," explained Rose. She poked about with her trowel and knife, trying to dig up some fresh soil to fill in the hole where the bowl had been.

"Mr Wotsit," she suddenly said, "would you like to see the bowl I found last time I was here?" Without waiting for an answer, she reached as far under the bushes as she could and pulled out the dirty bowl by one of its handles. "You see, it'll make a lovely bowl for my kitchen," said Rose. "I might use it to collect blackberries or nuts or flowers or something. Would you like to get a little of the dirt off it, Mr Wotsit?" She left him to it and went back to her digging. Suddenly, her trowel made that familiar rasping sound again. Something else was there, waiting to be part of her kitchen utensils! She scraped and poked and pulled around in the soil, and before long up came a sort of metal cup with a stem. It was rather like a wineglass, but it was made of metal and not of glass. The cup part was wide and the stem was thick and bumpy, and the whole thing was encrusted with soil and clay.

Rose was thrilled. "Oh, look, Mr Wotsit! Now we've got a sort of vase to go with the bowl! I'll put this on the grass next to you. Aren't we lucky? I'm going to dig again – p'rhaps there's something else here for my kitchen!"

She knelt down again, and within ten minutes she had pulled out a knobbly egg-shaped object and two round flat ones. "Something knobbly – and two plates, Mr Wotsit!" cried Rose, putting them carefully down on the grass under a gorse bush. She stood up stiffly after all that kneeling, shook each leg and then danced about with glee.

"Just wait till they come to my house-warming and see all the things I've found! I've had enough digging and I don't think there's anything else in the soil anyway. Now I'm going to go out collecting sticks for my bonfire."

She ran out of the den on to the hills. The Wotsit nodded absent-mindedly. He was engrossed in poking away the lumps of clay and dirt stuck to the bowl. They were gradually falling off as he jabbed away with the point of his tail, but it was hard work. The bowl must have been in the ground for a very long time.

"But who would have left their kitchen bowls and cups and plates in a hole in the ground?" His furry black forehead creased into a frown. "I must put my thinking cap on," he murmured to himself.

A rainbow-striped schoolboy's cap with a Little Elmford School badge appeared on the back of his black furry head. "Drat my magic!" he muttered in disgust. "Sometimes it's too clever for its own good!"

He tore the cap off and rammed it into the very middle of the nearest gorse bush. Then he sat down on the grass and, with feet, hands and pointed tail, energetically started work again on the objects Rose had dug up.

While Rose and the Wotsit were busy on Golden Hills, Mr Satterthwaite was at home in the School House, sitting in front of his television set watching a magazine programme. He was sprawled full length in a deep comfortable chair, and his eyes kept closing.

He hoped he would stay awake long enough to see the sports reports, but he was quite exhausted. Fatigued, as old Pamplemousse would say. It was extremely fatiguing to have another interview with Mrs Prissy Wagtail. She had just shrugged when he told her about the three new pupils.

"Three?" she had said, raising one eyebrow. "Only three? And gypsies, who might be moving on next week? It has to be twenty *at least*, Mr Satterthwaite, before we'll even consider keeping the school open after next year. And by the end of June don't forget!"

Mr Satterthwaite hadn't replied. How could he explain to her that mere numbers of children didn't make a school? "Small is beautiful," thought Mr Satterthwaite, dozing off again. He woke with a start a couple of minutes later, as he heard a familiar voice. What on earth did *he* want at this time of the evening? Perhaps he wanted to discuss tomorrow's menu – he took such pride in his job, did old Pamplemousse.

"Come in!" he called, struggling upright in his chair. But no one came in – and Satterthwaite realized that Pamplemousse's voice was coming from the television set! There he was in his usual spotless white coat and tall white hat – and surely that was Little Elmford School in the background of the picture.

Mr Satterthwaite wondered whether he was dreaming. The interviewer, a young lady in blue denim, was saying:

"So, Monsieur Pamplemousse, even though you work in a small village school, you still think that you have a good chance of becoming School Cook of the Year?"

"I think I am a most excellent cook," answered Monsieur Pamplemousse with a modest shrug. "I have cooked for royalty, for General de Gaulle, for the great people of the world! Now I am older I like to live in

England in a little village – but my skill and experience are used to tempt the appetites of the little ones." He smiled broadly: "And in this I am always successful." The young lady seemed to be at a loss for words. Monsieur Pamplemousse, however, was not. "You wish to ask whether I serve often the frogs' legs or the snails? Never, Mademoiselle, is the answer. For school dinners they are too expensive! I work always within a budget, I am a good housewife!" He laughed. "But perhaps you also wish to ask more about the competition?" he prompted.

"Ah, ah, yes ... er, thank you, Monsieur Pamplemousse."

"Well, all at first I must speak with my headmaster about it. I have not yet revealed to him my decision to enter the competition. But he is a charming gentleman, an excellent bloke."

Mr Satterthwaite was sitting up in his easy chair, mouth slightly open, unable to believe his eyes and ears.

"... I foresee no difficulties with Mr Satterthwaite. After all..." and here Monsieur Pamplemousse straightened himself up and became very serious: "... After all, I enter this competition not for the prize, the money: it is of no importance to me at all. No, no, it is because the children begged me – I enter this competition solely for the honour and glory of Little Elmford Village School – which is threatened with closure!"

The school chef faded from the screen, and Mr Satterthwaite found himself smiling hugely. "The old beggar!" he said aloud. "The artful old beggar!"

His telephone suddenly rang – probably one of his headmaster friends wanting to congratulate him on his wily old cook. He lifted the receiver.

"Mr Satterthwaite? How dare you get your school cook to take part in a publicity-seeking circus?" He might have guessed – Mrs Wagtail. She continued indignantly: "He had no right to do this, as one of our employees! I'm sure he won't be allowed time off his paid working hours to go in for this competition!"

"I'll see that he lets you have notification in writing first post tomorrow," promised Mr Satterthwaite. "After all, Mrs Wagtail – if he does well, it will be nothing but good publicity for the local authority who is not afraid to employ such an ... individualist."

"Hmmm," said Mrs Wagtail, not convinced, and he heard her put the receiver down.

"And nothing but good publicity for Little Elmford Village School, too!" he said to the telephone. "Pamplemousse, you old beggar, you've dropped a real 'bombe surprise'."

CHAPTER TWELVE

Miss Jelly Gets Excited

"MY TOOTH'S WOBBLY!" announced Erica suddenly at tidying-up time the next morning. "Look, Miss Jelly, my tooth's wobbly!" She bared her teeth at Miss Jelly. "Go on, you can have a wobble if you like!"

"It's bending right over," said Julie, peering into Erica's mouth.

"She looks like a shark, like Jaws!" said Pete.

"Like Dracula!" said Gavin.

"Our Nana hasn't got no teeth," said Trixie.

"Our Nana hasn't either!" cried lots of other people.

"Our Nana's got plastic teeth," said Desmond proudly. "She keeps them in a beer mug at night."

"My Dad's got plastic teeth, an' all," said Johnny, "and when he was working on the rigs he stood on the edge one day and his teeth fell in the sea, and a octopus swallered 'em..."

Miss Jelly decided that it was time for a change of subject. The children had worked hard all morning, so she was going to take them for a quick run on Golden Hills before dinner.

They went along the passage, sniffing deeply to

guess what Monsieur Pamplemousse had ready for them today.

"It's that cheese 'n' onion quiche," said Isabel, concentrating hard.

"P'raps we'll have that gooseberry snow for pudding," suggested Charlotte, "or baked Alaska!"

"Or fruit roly-poly!"

"Or choc ice 'n' chips!"

With these pleasant surmises in their minds they poured out of the school door into the breezy Spring sunshine. Golden Hills looked fresh and green, and the gorse was just beginning to show golden buds. Everywhere there seemed to be flocks of little birds, twittering or squabbling or simply flying from bush to bush to gossip.

The children ran up and down the grassy hills, as sure-footed as energetic little mountain goats. Miss Jelly walked round enjoying their enjoyment.

Rose suddenly ran up and pulled at her hand. "Miss Jelly, I've got a den. Come and see."

Miss Jelly strolled over with her to a far corner of the field. There was a semicircle of gorse bushes and Rose took her inside. At the further end was an area of freshly flattened soil, surrounded by stones.

"See, that's my fireplace, Miss Jelly," said Rose proudly. "My Mum and Dad and Barney are coming to see my den. I asked them. We're going to have a bonfire and a picnic. My Mum said we could. I made it all myself."

Miss Jelly looked round, "It's lovely, Rose! Did you find it all by yourself?"

"Yes, and I've got some things for my kitchen. I found them."

She dived on to all fours and reached under a gorse bush.

"Look, Miss Jelly, look what I've got . . ." She stood in front of her teacher with an armful of jumbled dirty metal objects.

"What are they for, Rose?" asked Miss Jelly, then bent down and peered at them. Rose was glad to see her suddenly look intensely interested. "Good heavens, Rose!" she said, holding the metal bowl close to her face and narrowing her eyes to examine it.

"Mr Wotsit helped me clean them a little bit," said Rose, "but they're still rather dirty." She chewed a plait anxiously as she waited for Miss Jelly's reply.

Miss Jelly pulled her hanky out of her pocket and wetted it in her mouth. Then she rubbed the side of the bowl gently but firmly.

"A-maz-ing!" breathed Miss Jelly. "It's red! It's coming deep red – look, Rose. That's a precious stone, Rose, I'm sure."

She held out the bowl for Rose to see. Where she had rubbed, there was now appearing an intricate pattern, like a band of silver thread woven under and over, in and out, worked into the actual metal. And in the centre of the pattern sat a large round stone which glowed a rich red.

"This must be a very ancient bowl, Rose! And what's that you've got there?" she asked, suddenly turning her eyes to the other objects in Rose's arms.

"That's . . . a goblet, a goblet, I'm sure!"

She gently put the bowl on the grass and nearly snatched the dirty-looking goblet from Rose's arms. Rose had seldom seen Miss Jelly so excited – perhaps not since that warm morning on which their moon moth had emerged from its chrysalis and had clung to the Wendy House wall to dry its beautiful wings.

"In-cred-ible!" whispered Miss Jelly, as she turned the goblet round and round in her hands. There was a faraway, almost wild look in her eyes.

"Miss Je-elly! Miss Je-elly!" A chorus of demanding voices was coming nearer. Miss Jelly quickly took all the objects from Rose into her own arms.

"What interesting things, Rose! I'm going to take them back to school to show Mr Satterthwaite – and perhaps at home-time you can bring me back here and show me *exactly* where you found them."

"But they're for my den!" protested Rose.

Miss Jelly said firmly, "I promise you, Rose, I'll get you something *much* nicer for your den next time I'm in Chesterby. But for now, I'd like to keep these very safe. I think you've found something extra special, and a lot of people are going to be very interested in these things."

She was cradling the metal objects in her arms as one might a baby.

Rose was surprised at Miss Jelly's excitement, but after a few months at school she was getting used to the funny ways of teachers.

"All right," she conceded. "You can keep them – but I'd like a doll's teaset, with a teapot, and a kettle, and saucepans."

Then she added as an afterthought: "Red plastic, please – that'll be much easier to clean than them what I found...."

When Rose's mother came to meet her after school, Miss Jelly went out to her at the gate.

"It's her last chance," Rose overheard her say

coaxingly. "Her last chance before they move in and take over the whole place. After that children won't be allowed near Golden Hills again to play." Did Miss Jelly mean the school *was* going to be closed and the bulldozers would soon be flattening Golden Hills? But at tea-time her mother told her that the house-warming would be celebrated that very evening. Somehow Miss Jelly had persuaded her.

As twilight thickened over the village and birdsong stilled, the Golden Hills were noisy with chatter and laughter. Word had gone round that there was to be some sort of party. Several of Rose's friends ran over, attracted by the roaring brilliance of the huge bonfire her father had got going. Smiling parents followed at a sauntering pace. Lupin loped up silently, pulling a home-made go-cart, and unloaded several logs and bundles of twigs. His twin sisters pulled handfuls of dry fir-cones from their pockets. "Great!" exclaimed Barney and Timpo, who were helping to feed the roaring giant.

Lupin unslung a sack from his back. "Taters," he said briefly. He showed Barney and Timpo how to prick them and push them forward right into the golden ashes, shielding their faces from the fierce heat. Rose's mother arrived with trays of roast sausages, and Rose danced round handing them out, offering the jar of mustard, chewing the hot parkin Miss Jelly had brought, and chattering to everyone and anyone. Columbine and Eglantine sidled up to Rose and curled some trails of honeysuckle round her ears and through her plaits. "From our Mam," explained Colly.

Mr Satterthwaite strolled over and pulled a large bag of striped humbugs from his pocket. Isabel took

one, then was overcome by emotion, let go of her mother's hand and disappeared behind a bush.

Monsieur Pamplemousse arrived carrying a huge crate of bottles. He placed it on the grass with a clatter. "Mr Adam has sent some Norberry spring water," he explained. "I shall serve it chilled, of course." He handed out bottles and straws with a beaming smile.

Richard and Graham Steel joined Barney, Timpo and Lupin and helped to keep the fire going with withered branches of gorse. "This is a super way to end our half-term," said Graham, his mouth full of parkin. "Oh, gosh, look – there's Monsieur Pamplemousse!" He rushed over to ask more about blowing up the bridge near Paris.

The Wotsit zoomed round in the flickering darkness, landing on people's shoulders and making them jump. "I don't think much of the food you're serving at your house-warming, polite little girl!" he screeched at Rose.

"Oh, Mr Wotsit!" said Miss Jelly reproachfully. She hastily felt in her pockets and pulled out some leftover stumps of white chalk. "Specially for you," she whispered to him.

"Aw, Miss Jelly . . . !" he said huskily, and zoomed off, crunching noisily.

At last the low flames flickered more slowly and parents began to take reluctant children home to bed. Goodbyes echoed across the Golden Hills. Rose jigged up and down excitedly in front of Barney and her parents, her plaits jumping with her. "That was a lovely, *lovely* house-warming!" she said. "Lovely, *lovely*!"

But when her mother was tucking her up in bed, she

burst into tears. "I don't want them to pull the school down," she sobbed. "You won't let the bulldozers come, Mam, you won't, will you? You won't let them flatten Golden Hills, will you? *Will* you?"

"Oh, Rose ..." whispered Mrs Battersby. "I don't know, I just don't know..."

CHAPTER THIRTEEN

Ten Down, Ten to Make

THE NEXT FEW days were unusually busy at Little Elmford School. Important-looking visitors carrying flat black brief-cases or armfuls of documents kept arriving. They would get out of their cars at the school gate, look round and stare as though hypnotized at Golden Hills (which Mr Satterthwaite had roped off), then find their way to his room.

Rose had had her house-warming just in time.

"They're people from the museums," explained Miss Jelly to her class. "They want to see the things Rose found. They are very, very old things, more than a thousand years old." She started to make chalk dots on the blackboard to show how many a thousand was. The class got tired of counting at two hundred and thirty-nine – but by then they knew that Rose's treasures were very old indeed.

"Are they really treasures, like what pirates nick on telly?" enquired Pete.

Miss Jelly nodded. "They really *are* treasures and there really were pirates! The people who lived in Little Elmford knew that some fierce Viking pirates had rowed across the sea in their dragon boats and had landed on the beach only ten miles away – someone must have galloped here quickly on horseback to warn them. So before they all escaped, they fetched their most precious treasures from the church. There was a beautiful gold and silver bowl, a chalice of gold (the one Rose thought was a vase), two ornamented plates, and a wonderful jewelled brooch, or clasp, which was only worn on very special occasions. The villagers and their priest..."

"Like what the vicar is?"

Miss Jelly nodded. "Yes. They quickly dug a hole at the side of the village, perhaps under a tree, and buried the treasures deep in the soil where no Viking could find them."

"What happened to the people in Little Elmford?" asked Isabel, anxiously wriggling.

"I think a few of the bravest young men stayed to fight the Vikings, and they got killed. But I expect the rest came back when the Vikings had gone. The Vikings had been furious when they found that there were no treasures to steal, so they set fire to everything: the huts where the people lived, the bushes and trees round the village, and even the church itself. When the people came back, there was nowhere to live. So the first thing they had to do was to start building their houses and their church all over again."

"Why didn't they dig up the treasures?" asked Desmond.

"I expect they thought they'd leave them hidden, just in case the Vikings came back. Then perhaps the months and years went by and they just forgot where the treasures were."

"Till I found them!" beamed Rose.

"I beg your pardon!" interrupted a high-pitched

shriek as the Wotsit zoomed across the room to land on Miss Jelly's table. "I think you mean until *we* found them, don't you, polite little girl?"

He stood there with his gaudy colours blazing, his furry black hands resting indignantly on his striped sides. "Yes, indeed!" he went on, to Miss Jelly and the class: "Yes, indeed! I was there with her as she played, and I said: 'Little girl, I have a feeling there's something of tremendous importance right there under those stones. Why don't you dig a little and see?' And as it turned out, my hunch was quite correct!"

Rose was listening open-mouthed. She swallowed. "But..." she began.

He went on airily. "'Yes,' I said, when I saw what she'd dug up, 'Yes, those are indisputably church treasures hidden from the ravages of the Vikings. Indisputably! Didn't I, m'dear?'"

Rose could only shake her head. She knew *she* had found them, alone, and she could see that Miss Jelly believed her too.

Gavin said slowly, thinking aloud, "Perhaps there's more treasures! More treasures what Rose *didn't* find!"

"Yes, indeed," said Miss Jelly. "Some of those people from the museum are going to dig up other bits of Golden Hills to see what else they can find. And they think perhaps parts of the burnt huts are under the hills and that's why they're so bumpy."

"And grass has growed over them," added Erica in agreement.

"When can we see them treasures again?" asked Johnny eagerly.

"They have to be properly cleaned..." began Miss Jelly.

"Yes, lucky I was on hand to start the process," chimed in the Wotsit. "It's the sort of delicate task you need an expert for. Of course, as soon as I saw they were part of an immensely valuable treasure trove, I advised the little girl to take them straight to someone in authority – didn't I, polite little girl?"

This time the polite little girl scowled horribly at the Wotsit and Miss Jelly said quickly: "When the people from the museum have examined the things and perhaps mended them, then cleaned and polished them, they have promised we can have them on show in school for a few days, just for Little Elmford to enjoy. After all – they used to belong to the village in the time of *your* great, great, great, lots-of-greats, grandparents!"

Miss Jelly was on duty at afternoon playtime. As she strolled in the early May sunshine with the children, she was surprised to see Mrs Williams, Mr Satterthwaite and Monsieur Pamplemousse coming out to join her. The headmaster was holding a large box which he opened as the children crowded round. "A celebration!" he announced, beaming.

"Sherbet fountains!" gasped everyone, turning to tell the news to the others pressing round from the back. In three minutes all the children and all the staff were sucking the liquorice straws and enjoying the bitter-sweet sherbet.

Even Monsieur Pamplemousse hesitatingly accepted one. "This English delicacy, I am not acquainted with it," he murmured. "I suck? I blow? The paper is edible?" The children soon instructed him in the art of attacking his first sherbet fountain.

Meanwhile Miss Jelly and Mrs Williams were wondering why their headmaster was suddenly acting like Father Christmas.

"It's those archaeologists!" he told them, beaming at such an unexpected stroke of luck. "A professor and three colleagues are coming to stay in Little Elmford for at least the whole of this summer to excavate Golden Hills. They're going to rent houses near the village and bring their families!"

Mrs Williams looked blank. Miss Jelly's eyes lit up. "Children!" she said.

"Yes, between them they've got seven children of primary school age – and they'll be coming to our school! Do you see, do you see?" Mr Satterthwaite sprayed an arc of sherbet through the air as he waved his arms to explain. "Seven more, plus the three Smiths – that'll be ten new children already. So I suppose there might still just be a faint chance of finding ten more by the end of June..." Then his brave smile faded as he looked anxiously at their faces. "What do you think...?"

CHAPTER FOURTEEN

Newcomers

IT WAS NEARLY the end of May, and the hawthorn bushes round Golden Hills were beginning to show white blossom. Gorse and broom bushes made brilliant golden patches against the grass, and the high-pitched tweeting of skylarks could be heard above the village all day long.

Although part of Golden Hills was now roped off so that the team of archaeologists could work undisturbed, the children still often crept as close as they could. They would lie on their stomachs to observe the careful digging and brushing that was going on, and to watch fascinated as "Rose's den" was meticulously staked out and photographed. Other sightseers were also finding their way to Little Elmford to see exactly where such a magnificent golden hoard had been found. The children of the school were even growing used to posing for press photographers and TV cameras.

Eglantine, Columbine and Lupin were still there, much to Mr Satterthwaite's relief: their parents seemed in no hurry to start their caravan rolling elsewhere. In fact, the headmaster had recently opened his door one misty morning to fetch in the milk, and had found a bottle of crimson elderberry wine and a pot of crabapple jelly on his step. He assumed they were a gift from the appreciative Smiths.

Lupin had made friends with Barney and Timpo. They spent a good deal of their spare time on Norberry Hill, exploring the hillside behind Mr Adam's house where the spring bubbled out from between the rocks, or simply talking to the old man. He would chat to them for hours about the ancient history of the village. Then he would encourage them to fill bottles with the icy spring water to take home. "It's too good to keep to ourselves," he would say.

"My Mum likes it," said Lupin. "She's always asking me to bring home more. She says it does her jijestion good."

"Pamp thought it was great when he tried it for the first time at Rose's house-warming," said Timpo. "He said it would be nicer than tap water to drink with school dinners."

"We should set up a stall and sell bottles of it!" joked Barney. "People might even pay us for it."

"In France they already do that," said Mr Adam. "Selling mineral water is big business."

The three boys looked at him thoughtfully. "Couldn't we do that?" asked Lupin hopefully. "My Mum and Dad used to sell things off a stall in Kent – cherries an' pears an' things."

"Who'd buy *water*?" said Timpo. "They've only got to go up Norberry Hill and get some for themselves, free!"

"Yes, but people are surprisingly lazy," mused Mr Adam, "they'd rather have it brought to their doors in handy bottles. You can buy bottled Malvern Water and Ashbourne Water – why not Norberry Hill Water?"

Timpo was still doubtful. "It would take us ages to fill even a dozen bottles from the spring – you know you have to push the moss and ferns to one side and kneel there for ages with wet knees, holding a bottle, while the water splashes out from the rocks."

Mr Adam knowingly put his finger alongside his nose. "Ah, but to fill hundreds of bottles we'd need a small plant."

The boys looked blank, but Mr Adam went on thinking aloud: "And for that we'd need to talk to that builder out at Green Acres."

"Mr Steel!" exclaimed the three boys together.

The old man looked faintly surprised. "Yes, that's right – do you know him already? Let's take a stroll over there now, then, shall we? We'll have a little chat with him about a small plant."

One morning during the same week, Julie, Jean and Charlotte presented themselves to Mr Satterthwaite. "We brung you some money," began Julie.

"To pay Miss Jelly and Mrs Williams and Pamp," went on Charlotte.

"Cos there's not enough money to pay them, an' them men in Chesterby are goin' to shut the school..." explained Jean.

"We been asking people for their change," said Charlotte, thrusting a heavy paper bag full of small change into the headmaster's hands.

"They give us lots," said Jean brightly.

"Comin' out the Umpire's Arms," smiled Julie.

"Why've they got to close the school? We want to stay here and be teached!"

"Yeh!" nodded the other two, looking up at Mr Satterthwaite. He looked down at them, not knowing what to say. He knew exactly what they were trying to tell him; he couldn't have put it better himself – but he didn't know the answer.

He looked into the paper bag. The heavy coppers would probably amount to only a few pounds. "I tell you what, girls," he said slowly. "Let's look on the bright side, shall we? We'll buy some bulbs with this money, and you three can help me plant them all round the school: red tulips, yellow daffodils and lots of little snowdrops. That'll give us all something to look forward to next spring. How about that?"

The three little girls nodded enthusiastically. "They wouldn't dare bulldoze our bulbs, would they, Mr Satterthwaite?" asked Julie, trustingly. Like Mrs Battersby, the headmaster could only shake his head and say slowly: "I don't know ... I just don't know ..."

Meanwhile, the archaeologists' children had arrived, all seven of them. The Professor himself brought Henry and Emma to the headmaster's room. Henry was tall and solemn-looking, and Emma was a quiet, pretty little girl; she was to join Miss Jelly's class.

Naomi and David also came to Miss Jelly that morning, while their big sister, Ruth, went to Mrs Williams. All three were pale-faced and dark-eyed. Naomi and David watched everything that went on in class, learning quickly how to fit in. At playtime the children gathered round the newcomers.

"Is your Dad going to dig up Golden Hills?" Timpo asked Henry.

"In a manner of speaking," said Henry loftily.

"Your Dad too?" Barney asked Ruth.

"No, not Papa – Mama is the archaeologist," said Ruth gravely. "Up until now she's been in charge of a dig in the desert."

"Why was she a-diggin' the desert?" asked Johnny with a frown.

"To uncover an ancient city," answered Ruth.

"Do you get wrynecks in this part of the country?" enquired Henry suddenly.

"Only as rare visitors," answered Lupin, equally unexpectedly.

Henry's solemn face lit up. "I say, have you a pair of binoculars? I'll bring mine and you can try them, if you like..." They sauntered off talking earnestly together.

Suddenly there was a squeal of brakes and a huge orange Cadillac stopped at the school gate in a spray of gravel. Out jumped two girls who looked about ten and eleven. They slammed the doors and waved to the driver of the car as it shot backward down the road and then screamed away past the Umpire's Arms.

The girls turned and strode gracefully into the school yard. There was a sudden hush as the other children took in their gloves, scarves, long trousers, fur jackets, fleecy boots, black hair and black faces.

"Say," said the taller of the two, "where's your school director?" No one answered. Some of Class I had never met anyone with a black skin before.

"C'mon, you kids," said the girl impatiently. "Where's the boss?"

Everyone suddenly stopped staring and rushed to take the two newcomers to Mr Satterthwaite.

During the next lesson the headmaster brought the two girls to Mrs Williams's room. He had an odd expression on his face.

"I'm sure you'll all find no difficulty getting to know Cynthia and Helen – " he began.

"Most people get to call us Sin and Hell!" broke in Helen cheerfully. "*She's* ugly as sin . . ."

"And *she*'s black as hell!" finished her sister with a delighted grin. The children gasped and looked to see what effect this was having on Mr Satterthwaite. But he was wearing his blankest expression and giving nothing away.

"Say, can't you get the heating on in here? It's like an ice-box," shuddered Cynthia, burrowing even further down into her fur jacket.

"You sure could do with some Mexican sunshine here," nodded Helen.

"Oh, have you had a holiday in Mexico?" asked Mrs Williams, conversationally.

"Four years," said Cynthia laconically.

"Pa was diggin' up an Aztec temple," said Helen.

"Skeletons everywhere," said Cynthia. "D'you know they killed human sacrifices by the thousand?" she asked the class, who sat as though hypnotized. "They used to march prisoners up to the altar, then while they were still alive, they would – "

Mr Satterthwaite tiptoed out. He felt that Sin and Hell would have few problems settling down at Little Elmford.

CHAPTER FIFTEEN

Important Letters

IT WASN'T LONG before the newcomers heard about the threat hanging over the future of the school. They were horrified.

"What are you going to do about it?" asked Ruth, her dark eyes full of concern. "This is such a friendly school – surely there's something someone can do?"

"Well, we had a Protest March," said Barney. "That made sure everyone knew what was going on, and gave Little Elmford School plenty of publicity. Although it didn't seem to make them change their minds," he added sadly.

"Pa says you should always go right to the top!" said Cynthia firmly. "Write to the President!"

"The Queen, stoopid!" said Helen, her black face shining up from the collar of a thick Aran sweater.

"All right, then – write to the Queen. She seems a real nice lady. She's got kids herself, hasn't she? I bet she'd 've been real upset if *their* school had been closed and they were bussed to another one."

"How do you start?" asked Helen, grabbing a piece of rough paper and a pencil. "Dear Queen?"

"Aw, Hell!" protested her sister. "No, it's Your

Dear Majesty – I think. Or is it Dear Your Majesty . . . ?"

"I think you address her as 'Ma'am'," said Henry gravely.

This was the version finally agreed upon:

TO THE QUEEN:
Dear Ma'am,
We are writing to you from Little Elmford School, Little Elmford. It is a small village school, but we are very happy here and so are our teachers. We think we are learning just as much as children in big schools in towns.

Now we have been told that our school will probably have to be closed because it is too small. Please can *you* make the Local Authority change its mind?

We await your gracious reply with eager anticipation,

Your devoted and humble subjects,
(*That last part was Henry's contribution*)
The pupils and staff of Little Elmford School

Everyone in the school wanted to sign the letter. Miss Jelly had to help a few of her class to write their names neatly.

"Oh, Jean, you've written 'naeJ' again," she sighed. "Still, I don't expect the Queen will mind."

"I've never written to Buckingham Palace before," said Liz, signing her name carefully.

"Me neither," said Di, putting her tongue between her teeth as she concentrated on writing Diana Gracie Fields Jones.

"You're not gonna send that letter to Her Maj.

without me signing it, now are you?" whooped the Wotsit when he realized what was going on. "*My* signature might just persuade her to use her influence. Purple chalk O.K.?"

"Certainly not!" snapped Henry, scandalized. He put on his most pompous voice. "You may put your ... mark there, look, *there*, down in that corner." The Wotsit scowled horribly at Henry.

"Isn't he just the cutest little thing when he's mad at someone?" said Cynthia. "Just look at that darling little green tongue he's sticking out at me!"

The Wotsit scowled even more horribly at her and took Henry's pen. He made an illegible scrawl on the corner of the writing paper. "There!" he said. "Her Maj.'ll be glad to see that the letter has *my* approval," he added airily, and zoomed off to look for an open stock cupboard.

In the end there were so many signatures that two extra pages had to be added. Eggy sidled up to Henry and said: "My Mum said, seeing as 'ow we was writing from the country, did you want some pressed flowers to put in with it?"

"Yes," added Mr Satterthwaite eagerly, "*I* was wondering whether our local cricket fixture list might interest Her Majesty – or indeed any others of the Royal Family; she might pass it round at breakfast, perhaps ..." But Henry was very firm: only the letter and the signatures were to be sent. And eventually – after all Miss Jelly's class had volunteered to lick the envelope – it was ready. The whole school turned out to cheer the postman (Gavin's father) as he pedalled heavily away with it in his bag.

School seemed humdrum for a few days after this,

but then something even more exciting occurred. Television crews were to visit the school yet again. But this time it was not the Little Elmford Hoard that interested them: it was the school chef, Monsieur Pamplemousse.

In the excitement following the Golden Hills find, the children had almost forgotten the School Cook of the Year competition. But at the end of May came a letter with the amazing announcement: Monsieur Pamplemousse was in the Final. The other finalist was the cook of Rexham Regis School, and the Final was to be filmed – at dinner-time – in only three days.

"Fantastic, Pamp!" cried Mr Satterthwaite, clapping the chef enthusiastically on the back, as though he were a fellow cricketer who had just made a century.

"Yes, you've gotta admit you're lucky I've been here to advise you all along," said the Wotsit, who happened to be cruising past. Monsieur Pamplemousse pursed his lips, and Mr Satterthwaite said hurriedly, "Er . . . Mr Wotsit, I rather think Mrs Williams is unpacking a new supply of coloured chalk – we do seem to be using it up rather quickly these days – perhaps you'd care to go along and give her a hand. . . ?"

The Wotsit hesitated; then greed won, and he made a U-turn in mid-air and zoomed back along the passage. Monsieur Pamplemousse hurried off to break the amazing news to Di and Liz.

The headmaster went to the school door, where a large packing case was being delivered. It was the Little Elmford Hoard, brought home for a few days so that the pieces could be put on display. He carried the packing case along to his room and locked the door behind him. He didn't want any silly jokes from that Wotsit – not just for the next few minutes. Very carefully he unpacked the gleaming pieces from their cocoons of tissue paper and wood shavings.

First to emerge were the two patens, shining silver plates with interwoven designs round the edge, ending in what looked like long, thin hounds' heads. Next he undid the chalice. Its polished gold gleamed and round the stem were set huge, glowing, dark red stones and knobs of shining blue.

The bowl appeared next. Round the top was a band of interlacing silver filigree patterns, set with jewels, and at each side was a silver handle, also patterned with the finest curls and spirals. Mr Satterthwaite whistled as he looked at all these treasures – he half wished *he* could have found them, not Rose.

He reached to the bottom of the packing case for the

last of all. It was in a small box. He opened it and gasped, remembering the dirty oval object Rose and Miss Jelly had shown him: only the dirt-encrusted pin on the back made them guess it was a clasp. But now – ! The golden fastening pin shone after its expert cleaning and inside a delicately wrought frame was the likeness of a man with a beard. His robes were enamelled in brilliant reds, blues and greens. The museum had enclosed a typewritten note: "This seems to be intended as a likeness of one of the early saints, possibly Barnabas."

For a full five minutes Mr Satterthwaite just sat and gazed at the thousand-year-old treasure. At last, with an incredulous sigh, he unlocked the school safe and carefully stored the Hoard away.

Then a thought struck him, and his eyes lit up. "Perfect!" he thought. "They can be on display during the Final of the School Cook Competition, the perfect background to the dining-room. One thing's for certain – Rexham Regis won't have anything to touch this!"

CHAPTER SIXTEEN

Monsieur Pamplemousse Conducts a Survey

"NO ONE'S MINDING US," said Gavin, looking round. There wasn't an adult in sight. It was half an hour before home-time, and the children had been brought to the dining-room by Timpo and Barney, who seemed to be in charge.

Suddenly the kitchen door opened and out stepped Monsieur Pamplemousse. Immediately there was a respectful silence. It was as though a great actor had stepped on to a stage. He stood and looked round at them thoughtfully. His overall was as dazzlingly white as ever – it never seemed to get dirty. And his tall white chef's hat seemed to stay upright on his head as though by magic.

"Good afternoon, children. I want you to help me with a little problem. Will you?"

"Yes!"

"Course we will."

"O.K."

"Yes, yes, Pamp!"

The chef held up his hand for silence. "Thank you, thank you, children. As you know, we have our School Cook of the Year Final in two days' time, and I know we shall all enjoy the occasion. But – " he stopped dramatically and looked at them all, then continued slowly – "*I still do not know what we shall eat!*"

"Ah!"

"Oh!"

There were gasps of consternation all round.

"So you see – I need your help, and quickly! We must think of a first course which you enjoy, followed by a second course which balances it. So, for instance, we do not enjoy banana fritters so much after fish in batter; and it is not suitable for plum pudding to follow meat pudding – you understand?"

The children nodded. Monsieur Pamplemousse looked at them again and asked rather resignedly: "I suppose you like best always fish fingers and chips?" The children closed their eyes and remembered the way he served those tiny, elegant French fried potatoes and golden fish fingers with a pretty little butterfly slice of lemon on them. They were delicious, but not always the best, by no means. "No!" they said.

"Ah?" The chef looked surprised. "Then perhaps you wish for roast chicken with herb stuffing and tiny bacon rolls?" The children shut their eyes again and breathed in deeply; they could almost smell the fragrant aromas. But that wasn't the absolute best. It was so hard to choose.

"We could have them little meat rolls with stuff inside, Pamp – "

"Yeah, them what you said was called larks wiv no 'eads."

"Yeah! Or that meat loaf an' your special tomato sauce..."

"Or chalk pie?" suggested the Wotsit, suddenly appearing.

"Or that stew wiv great hunks o' meat an' lots o' onions . . ."

"Yeah! Or grilled liver'n bacon 'n all those uvver fings what goes wiv 'm . . ."

There was a satisfied pause as everyone's mind was full of delightful pictures. Then Rose piped up: "Your salads are always pretty colours, Pamp."

The children reflected. Yes, Rose was right. "And it'll be on colour telly," pointed out Barney, backing up his sister.

"Yeah," agreed most people. "All them reds 'n greens 'n oranges 'n yellows – real pretty."

"Just like a box of coloured chalks!" said the Wotsit.

"Agreed then!" said Monsieur Pamplemousse firmly. "Now for the second course?"

"Ice-cream!"

"Cream doughnuts!"

"Treacle tart!"

"Trifle!"

"Christmas pudding!"

"Chalk crumble. . . !"

The chef covered his ears. "I cannot hear you all at once – you bruise my ears! Now remember: for the second course we want something filling that *every*one likes, something simple, perhaps something that your mothers make at home."

"Apple pie is what all Moms make, I guess," said Helen.

"Yes, our Mama does," nodded Ruth.

"An' mine!"

"An' ours!"

"And perhaps all mothers since Eve!" said

Monsieur Pamplemousse with a twinkle in his eye. "Very well then. It is settled. I thank you, children. You have aided me greatly. Now I must write out my order for ingredients – and many apples!"

CHAPTER SEVENTEEN

The Day of the Final

IT WAS 31ST MAY, the day of the Final. The children could hardly concentrate on their morning's work, but Monsieur Pamplemousse was very calm and spent his time directing his two "ladies" as usual.

Mr Satterthwaite, however, was a bundle of nerves. "It's like waiting to leave the pavilion to bat," he moaned to anyone who would listen to him. He visited both the classrooms two or three times, quite unnecessarily, sat down, stood up, went to the kitchen hatch, told feeble jokes to the TV team, paced the stone floor of the passage and twice nearly fell flat as he tripped over the cables of the TV cameras.

"He's a menace," growled Len, the chief technician, to Ben, his second-in-command. "Can't you do something about him?"

Ben went and leant through the hatch to the kitchen. He had a quiet word with Monsieur Pamplemousse, who came out of the kitchen with a tumbler full of sparkling liquid. Mr Satterthwaite looked at it, shrugged, and obediently tossed it back. Within moments he meekly retired to his study to recover from the effects.

"What was in that, then?" asked Len in amazement.

"Adam's Ale and my own secret ingredient..." murmured the chef, laying a finger alongside his nose and winking.

Ben and Len had already taken film of the Little Elmford Hoard as it stood, gleaming and glowing, on a dark blue velvet stand at one end of the room. A security man tried to hover inconspicuously nearby, pretending to be an electrician working at a socket.

Mrs Williams had lured the Wotsit into her stock cupboard to "count the coloured chalks". He had willingly obliged and was now happily locked in there.

At last it was dinner-time. The children walked into the dining-room as usual with their teachers. As usual there were small glasses of flowers in the centre of the tables laid for eight. As usual, there was a large menu card pinned up near the hatch, written in the chef's exquisitely elegant French handwriting. Today it read:

MENU

1. Little Elmford salad
   (shredded lettuce, garnished with chopped mint, parsley and chives, a variety of fresh vegetables, including diced beetroot, chopped tomatoes, grated carrot, sliced mushrooms).
   Honey roast ham.
   Mayonnaise *Granary bread*
2. Pamplemousse Pie
   (English Bramley apples in French pastry, sprinkled with flaked nuts and brown sugar)
   Whipped cream
   Sparkling Adam's Ale served with the meal.

Mrs Williams read the menu aloud for the benefit of those who could not yet decipher French handwriting.

Mr Satterthwaite walked in carefully. He didn't feel like any dinner after swallowing whatever it was old Pamplemousse had given him, but he normally ate with the children, and the TV people had stressed that everything was to be as usual. He sat down in an empty place between Johnny and Columbine. Barney, Henry, Cynthia, Ruth, Timpo and some of the other older children went to the hatch for the serving bowls and made sure each table had every item on the menu. Then they sat down and helped the younger children at their tables.

"I like this mint," said Johnny, picking up the green salad in his fingers.

"I seen Pamp out early in the fields this morning," remarked Columbine. "I seen him picking something."

"'Erbs, I spex," said Eglantine.

Erica wasn't too sure whether she liked grated carrot; she moved it round a little with her fork. "Come on, eat up," urged Mr Satterthwaite. "*I* like carrots. They make your hair curl, you know." Erica glanced doubtfully at the headmaster's almost bald head and decided to turn her attention to the ham instead.

"We 'ave 'am at 'ome," said Johnny, "but it's always in fin slices, not big 'n fick, like these." He chewed appreciatively.

The Pamplemousse Pie was delicious, and most people's hands went up for a second slice. The two kitchen ladies smiled at the children's eager faces as they refilled their plates. "You not full up *yet*?" they teased. The television cameras had been forgotten, and the atmosphere was as chatty and relaxed as usual.

When everything had been cleared away and the children had gone out to play, Monsieur Pamplemousse led Len, Ben and the other members of the television team into the kitchen, where places had been set for them and the same menu prepared. They all agreed it was a meal to remember.

"And now, Liz and Di, my dears," said Monsieur Pamplemousse, "I must go and prepare myself. They wish to helicopter me to the Television Centre, London, in order to be present at the Judging. I leave everything in your four good hands. Au revoir!"

CHAPTER EIGHTEEN

School Cook of the Year!

THAT EVENING EVERYONE in Little Elmford was watching *the* programme. In their caravan Colly, Eggy and Lupin were glued to a dilapidated portable their Dad had somehow managed to get working. For once the professor and his colleagues decided not to continue digging up history but watch it being made instead; their children made sure they got home in good time, so as not to miss a moment. Even old Mr Adam, who hadn't a set of his own, was sitting with Mr Steel and his wife as an honoured guest. The Steel boys had bribed everyone in the common room at Trafalgar Towers with toffees, and were grudgingly permitted to turn from "Sporting Superstars" to the other channel.

Barney and Rose were sitting excitedly with their mother in front of the television, waiting for the programme to start. Their father came in with an armful of bottles and rustling bags from the Umpire's Arms.

"Ooh, bagsy the roast chicken flavour!" said Barney, greedily diving on the bags of crisps.

"What about Cocky Locky?" asked his father slyly.

"Ah, yes, mmmm. . . ." Barney hesitated. "Right

then, I'll have tomato sauce flavour."

"Salt and vinegar for me, please," said Rose. "And can I have some of your mineral water, Mum?"

Her mother poured her a glassful, saying "Sssh, look, it's just going to start. Now I don't want to miss a *moment* of this, so don't interrupt!"

"It's not as nice as Adam's Ale," said Rose after a sip or two. "Not half as nice. And fancy, people pay for this and we can get Mr Adam's spring water free!"

Barney looked at his sister thoughtfully, a bright orange crisp half-way to his mouth. "Mr Steel and Mr Adam both think – " he began.

"Sssshh!" said their mother again. "It's starting!"

"Hi, fans!" shrilled a voice. "Your door was half open, so I guessed you'd left it for me!"

"SSSHHH!!!" hissed four furious voices together. For once the Wotsit took a hint and sat down quietly on the mantelpiece.

The teachers and Monsieur Pamplemousse's two dinner ladies were gathered in front of the headmaster's television set in the School House. At last came the moment the whole district was waiting for.

"Now for the films of the two finalists in our School Cook of the Year Competition! First we show you Monsieur Pamplemousse in action at Little Elmford Village School, then you will see Mrs Katy Cook (yes, that *really* is her name, ha ha, what a coincidence!) of Rexham Regis. And last of all you will see the chief of our judging panel, who will give you reasons for the final verdict."

The film began. The viewers in Little Elmford were fascinated to see themselves and their familiar surroundings on the television screen.

"Don't the tables and the flowers look nice?"

"Just look at that fabulous gold, doesn't it set everything off?"

"Ooh, look at Mr S. – he does look a bit under the weather, doesn't he?"

"But look at Chef – doesn't he look ... authoritative?"

"Distinguished, I'd say, Di."

"Oh, that Johnny Thompson, I wish he wouldn't eat everything with his fingers! The times I've told him ..."

"Ooh, look – fancy them taking a close-up of me just opening my mouth for that spoonful of pie!"

"You can just see a corner of our red Post Office frieze – look, there behind Barney and Timpo."

"Mmm, and I've still got pale red feet," murmured the headmaster.

"And there's that Isabel trotting out in the middle as usual! She'd only been ten minutes before!"

They all sat forward eagerly, enjoying every detail. And then it was the turn of Rexham Regis and Mrs Katy Cook. Rexham Regis was a very large primary school, and there had to be two dinner sittings, so from the very beginning Mrs Katy Cook, tall and thin, was under pressure.

Children filed into the large bare dining-hall, picked up their two plates each and moved them along the counter. Seven kitchen ladies in pink uniforms stood shoulder to shoulder. The first four doled out large helpings of steaming steak and kidney pie, carrots, peas and potatoes. The fifth pink figure poured a splash of gravy onto each plate. The last two in the line gave out generous portions of Spotted Dick and custard – Dollop-dollop-dollop-dollop-splash-dollop-splash!

Tall dark Mrs Cook remained calm throughout two sittings, reminding the kitchen staff to fill up the water jugs, making sure that fresh trays of steaming food were brought immediately they were needed, and always keeping the essential washing and drying up going smoothly at the back of the kitchen.

Di and Liz, viewing in Little Elmford, were open-mouthed at the gigantic scale of the operation.

"Not like our kitchen, is it, Liz?"

"You can say that again, Di!"

Then the judges were introduced, all distinguished in their own area of catering or cookery. There was a ten-minute pause for judging. Meanwhile the two finalists were seen chatting to the compere of the programme. Mrs Cook looked confident in a dark green dress. Monsieur Pamplemousse was quietly relaxed in a cream safari suit and discreet navy neckerchief. His silver hair shone under the lights.

"Ooh, doesn't he look lovely, Liz?"

Di and Liz clung to each other, thrilled to bits.

The chief judge returned. Mr Satterthwaite puffed away at his pipe in a fury of suspense. You could have heard a pin drop.

"From the first," began the chief, "we recognized that Mrs Cook had a much more difficult task with her huge numbers. But in spite of that her operation ran very smoothly, her choice of dishes was very British, the food was piping hot, there was plenty of it, and the children will have felt they were well fed. Mrs Cook gets full marks for organization and efficiency.

"However, we feel that Monsieur Pamplemousse in

Little Elmford added an extra ingredient to his dinners: imagination.

"The flowers, the menu, the serving of the local mineral water, the choice of dishes, the contact of staff with children, all made his dinner a little more of a social occasion. The choice of dishes, in particular, was excellent – not too unusual, and yet quite balanced. (Mrs Cook did serve two rather 'stodgy' items, remember.) Some of the children at Little Elmford did some 'consumer – ha ha – research' and advised their chef on his choice of dishes. And admirably they did it too, for they will have left the table feeling satisfied and yet not over-full."

He went on to make a few more points, then paused and said: "So, our choice of School Cook of the Year must be – Monsieur Pamplemousse!"

The noise in Mr Satterthwaite's sitting room was echoed all over Little Elmford, shrieks and yells of jubilation, mingled with clapping and stamping. Di and Liz sat on the settee sobbing with joy. Mrs Williams and Miss Jelly leaped up and down, clapping madly. Mr Satterthwaite found himself sitting on the table opening a bottle of champagne.

"Sssssshh!" he said, leaning forward to the set again.

There on the screen was their chef, modestly reaching out for a cheque, a beautifully engraved glass bowl, and a wooden spoon with a bow of golden ribbon round it.

"Well done," said the chief judge. "Well done, Monsieur Pamplemousse! – You certainly know your onions!"

CHAPTER NINETEEN

A Family Outing for the Steels

MR STEEL STEERED his rather muddy Land Rover off the main road and on to the gravel drive. Stone chippings spat from beneath the wheels and showered into the gloomy rhododendron bushes on either side. His wife glanced at the familiar notice as they slowly crunched past:

TRAFALGAR TOWERS
Preparatory School
for the sons of British Gentlemen

"I do hope both the boys can come out with us – Graham was kept in last time we visited, do you remember? Silly boy – fancy tying Mr Snood's shoelaces together while he watched the concert!"

Mr Steel snorted absent-mindedly. He was trying to find a place to park on the wide curve of drive in front of the main entrance. So many gleaming Mercedes, Jaguars, Volvos and Morgans had already been rather carelessly parked by other visiting parents that he had to drive further round, almost as far as the stable block.

They left the Land Rover and walked back to the main school. Two figures in green and yellow striped blazers appeared between the pillars at the top of the steps, and Mrs Steel waved. "Yoo-hoo, Richard! Graham!"

"For heaven's sake, you'll embarrass them," hissed Mr Steel. The boys came carefully down the steps and walked rather stiffly across to their parents.

"Hi!" said their father.

"H'lo," said the boys shyly.

"We having lunch out?" asked Graham.

Their mother nodded, smiling. "Of course!" It was three weeks since she had seen the boys, but she knew she mustn't overdo her delight at seeing them again.

"Old Snood's looking for you," said Richard in a low voice.

"What've you done this time?" asked his father resignedly.

"Well, someone showed me how to make water bombs with paper, you see..."

"Yes – and?"

"Well, I made a great one and filled it with water, but then Matron suddenly came round the corner, and the only way I could get rid of it..."

"Yes?"

"Well... was out of the window. So I just threw it."

"It was fab, Dad, it really was!" burst out Graham. "I was just coming in from the nets and I saw this thing hurtle out of the window – and guess who it landed on – SPLAT!"

"It *was* an accident," protested Richard. "Anyway, Old Snood always has it in for me. He found blobs of chewing gum on the tail of his gown yesterday and accused me straight away."

"Goodness!" said Mrs Steel. "Let's get going before

– oh dear" – she lowered her voice – "I do believe he's caught us anyway ..." The two boys stiffened.

A plump, busy little man hurried down the steps towards them. His black gown flew out behind him like flapping wings.

"Ah, good day, Mrs Steel, Mr Steel! Or should I say 'good afternoon'?" He glanced at his watch. "Just after twelve twenty-three, I see."

"We're just taking the boys out for a meal – our three-weekly visit," said Mrs Steel rather feebly.

"Ye-ers ..." said Mr Snood, his expression becoming frostier. "I think Steel One here knows he is very lucky to be permitted to join the family party." He spoke over Richard's head as though he weren't there. "Recently I have had grave doubts about his behaviour. We do try to keep high standards at Trafalgar Towers, and Steel One often falls far short of those requirements, I'm afraid." His glance slid round to Graham. "Now Steel Two has been a fairly reasonable young chap, *so far*..."

"Oh dear," murmured Mrs Steel. She wondered whether she should say she was sorry about the water bomb and hoped it hadn't ruined his suit, but she thought that perhaps wouldn't be very tactful.

Mr Snood was continuing: "Ye-ers, we think Steel Two *may* become a creditable Trafalgar Towers chap – he's fairly plucky at the nets, but he'll have to keep plugging away in the swimming baths. Bit of a booby on the diving board still, eh?"

A weak smile flickered across Graham's face. Out of the corner of his eye Mr Snood noticed a Range Rover draw up. "Ah, the Tunbridge-Browns have arrived – I won't detain you longer. We'll expect the boys back for seven o'clock sharp. Matron's customary Saturday evening buffet supper..."

"Rock bun and cocoa," muttered Graham.

Mr Snood flapped away to the Range Rover, then suddenly turned in his tracks and bustled back. "I quite forgot, Mrs Steel; Matron has asked me to mention that we do insist on name-tapes sewn on to *each* of the boys' dozen handkerchiefs."

At last the Steels drove away. "Shall we go to The Spinning Wheel or Jayne's Pantry?" asked Mr Steel.

"Jayne's Pantry!" answered the boys together.

"They give you bigger helpings," explained Graham. "And there aren't so many Traf boys there."

But when they entered the small restaurant there were several family groups that included boys wearing the Trafalgar Towers green and yellow blazers. "Find a corner table," whispered Richard, but there were no corner tables left, so they had to sit conspicuously in the centre of the room. They could hear scraps of conversation from the nearby tables.

"How's the Latin coming on, darling?"

"Next term can I have a bigger tuck box? I've finished all the tuck you gave me and Matron's fined me all of next week's pocket-money because I tore a hole in one of her blankets..."

"The girths were loose and I swung round under its belly..."

"But *why* were you all doing cross country through pouring rain?"

Graham whispered to his mother: "How's Squeaker?"

She didn't look at him. "I'm sorry, dear, I think she might be a *little* bit off her food."

"But I *told* you what to give her: fruit and tomatoes and dried food sometimes, and celery – she loves celery . . ."

Graham's voice had risen, and he realized that he was the only one in the room talking. He reddened and looked at his mother pleadingly.

"I'm sorry, darling," she whispered, "but I've been so careful to feed her and put her out in her run sometimes. Guinea pigs aren't terribly robust little animals, you know."

Graham's eyes filled. "But you *said* you'd look after her if I went away to school, you *promised*."

Mr Steel bit his lip and turned to Richard. "Anything interesting happening at school at the moment?"

"Only reports," answered Richard gloomily.

"Mine'll be awful."

Mr Steel looked from one of his sons to the other. Whenever they had a few hours together as a family both boys seemed irritable and despondent. "I sometimes wonder why we make this hundred-mile-round trip every three weeks," he said aloud. "Your mother and I only seem to depress you two boys when we visit."

"*You* don't depress us," said Richard. "It's just that you remind us of home."

"Well, I don't know why we bother to send you to Trafalgar Towers, in that case," said his father, exasperated.

"*Ed*ward!" cried his wife. "You're the one who's always insisted that they went away to your old school. *I*'d much rather they were at home with us all the time!"

"So would we! So would we!" cried the boys. Everyone else in Jayne's Pantry had stopped eating and was listening in fascination.

Mr Steel looked from his sons' faces to the pleading expression in his wife's eyes. Then he said slowly: "I might have a word with Mr Snood when we take you two back this evening – but meanwhile, is it to be sausages and chips, bacon and chips, or beefburger, beans and chips?"

CHAPTER TWENTY

Adam's Ale Saves the Day

IT WAS ALMOST the end of June. After the discovery of the Hoard, and Monsieur Pamplemousse's success, Little Elmford was on the map at last. There was a constant trickle of sightseers to Golden Hills, and often people would peer into the school yard, hoping for a glimpse of the now famous French chef.

But the future of the school was more uncertain than ever, and parents, teachers and governors were growing more and more depressed about their chances of keeping it open after the end of term. None of the publicity seemed to have helped at all.

Even the arrival of The Letter had made no real difference. Everyone had crowded forward to peer at it the day it had arrived in its stiff white envelope with a crimson royal crest on the back. Henry had carefully smoothed it out, mounted it on cardboard and hung it in the dining-room.

"Just look!" breathed Helen. "All She needs at the top of the letter is 'Buckingham Palace' – no street or house number or anything, and She knows we'll know straight away who it's from..."

Henry stood on a chair and read it aloud to the whole school. "'Her Majesty has asked me to say how much she regrets that she is unable to delay the closure of Little Elmford School, which sounds delightful. However, she sends her best wishes for the future to the staff and pupils.' Then a Lady-in-waiting has signed it."

"A Lady-In-Waiting!" repeated Cynthia, savouring each word.

"And Her Maj. may even have touched it Herself!" said Helen, quite awestruck.

"When she popped down the street with it to the post-box!" grinned Lupin.

But nothing else happened to cheer up the staff, and the children were unhappy about the prospect of leaving their familiar school and teachers.

"What will you do without us?" asked Isabel, looking at Miss Jelly with plaintive green eyes. Miss Jelly couldn't answer; she didn't know.

The week before, the headline in the *Chesterby Chronicle* had read

LITTLE ELMFORD SCHOOL THREATENED WITH CLOSURE

Yesterday's edition was headed:

LITTLE ELMFORD SCHOOL TO CLOSE SOON

"So *they* think it's a certainty," Mr Satterthwaite thought bitterly. He mopped his tanned brow and bald patch. Little Elmford was suffering from one of the longest heat-waves anyone in the village could remember. The adults had no energy for anything and the children were droopy and listless – only Cynthia and Helen shone with health and loved the heat.

"There's really only one place to be on a day like this," thought Mr Satterthwaite, closing his eyes. He imagined himself sitting in the sun with a straw hat tipped well over his eyes, shirt-sleeves rolled up, score card in his hands, hearing the thwack of ball on bat, the buzz of comment, the polite clapping. How fragrant the grass would smell! How blue the sky! How picturesque the white figures moving against the green...

"Hiya, Satty!" came a shrill screech from the open window. Mr Satterthwaite shot upright in his umpire's chair. The Wotsit flew swiftly across the room and landed on top of "Sunset over the Oval", which began to swing ominously.

"Mind my picture!" yelled Mr Satterthwaite.

"Hey, hey, Satty, you not feeling too good? Got outa bed the wrong side, huh? Well, that happens to the best of us, even me! Now, pin back your ears, Satty, old chap – have I got news for you! And you'll never believe it, but your Barney Battersby is at the bottom of it all!"

Mr Satterthwaite leant back weakly in his chair, mopped his forehead again and closed his eyes. The Wotsit jumped neatly on to his table and began to talk fast and excitedly into the headmaster's ear.

Mr Satterthwaite suddenly opened his eyes wide, sat up, leant forward to grasp exactly what the Wotsit was telling him, then smiled an incredulous smile.

"Good for old Steel!" he said. "And those lads in Class 2 – they should go far! Up on Norberry Hill, did you say? This should stump those number-counters in the Education Office! Perhaps this will bowl them out for once!"

It was the last day of June, and the weather was still scorching. The children didn't want to play out of doors, they preferred to stay inside in the cool of the old stone building with its flagged floors. Monsieur Pamplemousse left large jugs of chilled Adam's Ale in the dining-room, so people could help themselves during the day. His engraved bowl and prize wooden spoon were now proudly on show there, where the Little Elmford Hoard had been displayed before.

Now it was ten two. The last governors' meeting of the term – "Perhaps the last, ever?" thought Mr Satterthwaite – was due to begin at two o'clock. He was dreading the next hour, in spite of what the Wotsit had told him.

Neither Miss Jelly nor Mrs Williams had much energy or enthusiasm this afternoon. They knew what the governors' meeting was about, and they knew only too well what Mrs Wagtail's ultimatum had been.

"As it's Friday, and you've worked so well this week," announced Mrs Williams, "I think we'll give ourselves a treat and have a games afternoon." Small groups began playing Scrabble, Monopoly, Mastermind, Happy Families, chess, Snap and draughts. Mrs Williams wandered round among them, trying not to let her worry show on her face.

Class 1 were playing too – in the Wendy House, in the Lego, in the sand. Miss Jelly thought of the governors' meeting and the closure of the school and having to say goodbye to everyone. She began to sniff, and a slow tear rolled down her cheek and on to her dress. She joined the group in the water-play area, where everyone got splashed and her tears would go unnoticed.

"Two o'clock!" said Mrs Priscilla Wagtail

triumphantly, looking pointedly at her watch. The others in the room said nothing. They were listening to the sounds outside the school: birdsong, a lawnmower, an aeroplane droning, the distant crow of a rooster (Cocky Locky?), and – at last – the crunch of bicycle tyre on gravel. Five minutes later they heaved a sigh of relief as the vicar opened the door and stood smiling at them all.

"I don't know how the rest of you always beat me to it!" he beamed apologetically. "I just had to get Monsieur Pamplemousse's advice on pigs' trotters for my wife."

Mrs Wagtail pursed her lips and glanced again at her watch. "The meeting opened at 2.08 p.m.," she wrote at the top of her page. "Everyone *finally* present...."

"Good afternoon, everyone," began Mr Satterthwaite. "Thank you for coming. Perhaps Mrs Wagtail would like to speak first and tell us the school's position with regard to the number of children on roll."

"Yes indeed," said Mrs Wagtail, "I will be very brief. Little Elmford Village School was given until the last day of June – today – to find twenty more pupils. Otherwise the Local Education Authority would definitely close the school next year. We have been over the figures very carefully, and we find that only ten new children have joined you this year. Therefore there is no reason why this school should not definitely close."

Silence.

The vicar and Mrs Battersby looked at Mr Satterthwaite, who looked at Mr Steel. Eventually Mr

Steel said: "Perhaps, Mrs Wagtail, I am in possession of some new facts which will change your attitude."

"It is the attitude of the whole Education Committee," she answered primly.

"Then the Planning Department hasn't been in touch with you?"

"Planning Department?"

"About Adam's Ale?"

"Adam's Ale? That *water*? What's that got to do with it?"

Mr Satterthwaite reached out for the jug on the tray on his desk and poured a glassful of sparkling liquid. He offered it to Mrs Wagtail, who had been so floored by Mr Steel's questions that she drank it all.

"Yes, yes, pleasant enough," she admitted, "but what's it to do with closing the school?"

"I think it may be the reason for *not* closing the school," said Mr Steel. "After a couple of long conversations with young Barney Battersby and his friends, Timpo and Lupin, I decided to investigate the possibility of bottling this delicious water to sell. It appeared to be a sound financial risk, so after consultation with the Planning Department, I now have permission to build a small water-bottling plant at the foot of Norberry Hill. The building will be hidden from sight by the fir plantation there, since my partner in the venture, Mr Adam, is most concerned that it shall not spoil the look of the village. We shall employ six men, who will live in the village. Some of them will rent the new houses my firm has just finished beyond Ten Acre Field. They will be moving in soon and eight of their children will be of primary age and will come to Little Elmford School."

He paused. There was a long silence, finally broken by Mrs Wagtail.

"B-but that still only makes eighteen children. Two more would still be needed for the Council even to *consider* allowing the school to stay open."

"Yes," nodded Mr Steel. "Since my interest in this school began, I've been finding out what a splendid place it is – I needn't point out all its merits to you, Mrs Wagtail, you must know them already as a governor. But apart from its enthusiastic teachers, what other village school has its own archaeological site? In such beautiful surroundings? Can there be a better school cook? Can there be happier children? In fact, the school has so many advantages (quite apart from the fact that there are no fees!) that I can't think why I didn't send my own two children here the moment we moved to Little Elmford. If you can't beat 'em, join 'em! So next term (with Mr Satterthwaite's permission) there will be two young Steels here too – Graham and Richard!"

"Which makes twenty!" said Mrs Battersby jubilantly, speaking for the first time. Mr Satterthwaite slowly nodded his head in delighted amazement.

"We-ell... well..." said Mrs Wagtail, quite deflated. "Well, I suppose this does make one see things in a different light. I'd better report back to my committee. If you'll excuse me, I'll go now and put my thinking cap on!"

As she stood up to go, a large orange bath cap appeared on her head. She put her hand to her head, wrenched off the frilly plastic cap and looked at it in horror.

"This school gets madder and madder!" she snapped, and threw the cap straight out of the window. "If I had my way, I'd shut it tomorrow. But as I can't do that, I intend to resign instead. Little Elmford Village School can fight its own battles in future – without me!"

CHAPTER TWENTY-ONE

Class 1 Magic Again

THE LAST DAY of term arrived. It was brilliantly sunny and everyone was already in a holiday mood.

Mr Satterthwaite was out on the village cricket pitch with the older children. He was batting and they were all fielding, except Timpo who was bowling. The headmaster was extremely happy. He could think of no greater end-of-term treat for the children than to be out on the cricket field, in the sunshine, watching a master batsman at work.

Thwack! He knocked the ball firmly to the boundary. Two of the girls squeaked and leapt out of the way as it zipped past them.

"Bother! Dropped my daisy-chain!" grumbled one of them. Barney eventually stopped the ball half-way across the car park of the Umpire's Arms.

Ruth and Helen didn't even look up. They were sitting on the boundary line, watching Cynthia varnishing her toe-nails. "Who wants to play poor man's baseball, anyway?" she murmured, concentrating on her big toe.

Mr Satterthwaite sent the next ball sailing towards the churchyard. It crashed into one of the ancient yew trees. A family of blackbirds shot out of the greenery in all directions, squawking with fear. Henry pushed up his glasses thoughtfully to watch them.

The headmaster leant on his bat and closed his eyes contentedly. The school was definitely not to be closed. All his problems had somehow sorted themselves out. That left only one fly – or rather Wotsit – in the ointment. However, he did have the words of that Class 1 spell. He was pretty confident that spells spoken backwards worked backwards, so it should be easy to send the Wotsit packing when he became unbearable. Mmmm ... this sunshine was marvellous – this was the life...

"If it isn't Satter the batter!" shrieked a well-known voice. Mr Satterthwaite opened his eyes fast and furiously, just in time to see Timpo's next ball whizz past his leg and slam neatly into the middle stump.

"Howzat!" yelled every single child as with one voice. Mr Satterthwaite began to snarl at the Wotsit, but remembered just in time that he always told the children cricket was a gentleman's game. He managed a wintry smile of congratulations for the beaming Timpo and handed over the bat.

"What do you want *now*?" he hissed to the Wotsit, as he walked back to his Umpire's chair which had been placed in readiness under the trees.

The Wotsit danced about frenziedly in front of him at eye-level.

"It's like this, Satty, I've been thinking. First of all, I got all that good publicity for you by finding all that old gold."

"You?" asked the headmaster, puzzled.

"Sure. Then I pushed old Pamplemousse into that TV jamboree to show off his posh nosh...."

"You did?" asked Mr Satterthwaite weakly, feeling for the back of his chair and sitting down with a bump.

"Then I suggested that old man Steel should do what he oughter with the water...."

"*You* did?" asked the headmaster, completely bewildered. Had it really been like that?

"Sure. Get-up-and-go-man, that's me! The chap with the zap! The thing with the zing!" He did a little silent tap-dance in mid-air. "You didn't want your school to close, so you got that nice Miss Jelly to magic me here ..."

"I did?"

"Sure. You knew I was the man to sort out that kinda knotty problem..."

"I did?"

"And that's just what I've done. So ... and now I've got to break this to you real gentle, like, as I know you'll be upset – I gotta go."

"Go?"

"Yeah, sorry to have to tell you so sudden, like, but my time's up. Once I've been called out on a job and got all the problems sorted out, then I gotta push off again."

"You g-gotta push off? L-leave?" stammered Mr Satterthwaite, not daring to believe his ears.

"Yeah, I sure am sorry, Satty – I know you'll all miss my know-how round here, but duty's duty: I gotta go."

Mr Satterthwaite gulped and bit his lips to stop himself cheering. "Then you'd better go quickly," he said in a choking voice, "So it's not too upsetting..."

"Right, Satty, I sure am sorry. Well, I gotta go the way I came, so I'll nip in and see the Jelly babies, then be off. Incidentally, I might drop by some day and show these kids how cricket *really* should be played – but until then, I'll just say: cheerio, Satty, old chap, I'm glad we got on so well together..."

In school the classroom walls had all been stripped for the cleaners, and everything had been tidied away into cupboards.

"It don't look nice no more," remarked Johnny, looking round. "I don't like it all tidy."

"Wait till after the holidays," said Miss Jelly reassuringly. "We'll start to decorate the walls and make everything untidy again."

Class 1 were drawing some pictures for Miss Jelly to take home for the holidays to remind her of them.

"What a lovely horse," said Miss Jelly, looking at Gavin's drawing. "But he's green – I bet you've never really seen a green horse?"

"Yes, I have, last Monday."

"Where?"

"In the park, chasing the birds."

"Oh," said Miss Jelly and passed on to Erica's picture. "What's that, Erica?"

"That's my rabbit with nine baby rabbits."

"You've drawn the hutch very nicely, but where are all the rabbits?"

"They've gone for a walk; they'll be coming back to the hutch when their porridge is cool."

Jean shook Miss Jelly's arm. "Look, Miss Jelly, mine's a snow-storm." She drew some more purple spots on her paper. "And here's a Neskimo going home."

"Where does he live?" asked Miss Jelly.

"Look, there, *you* know, in his wigloo!"

"Ah," said Miss Jelly, nodding. She felt a hand tugging at her skirt.

"Canna goat the . . . ?" Miss Jelly nodded automatically.

"Hiya, Jelly babies!" came a shrill screech from the window-sill. The Wotsit had just landed there and was recovering his breath, one furry black hand on a heaving striped chest.

"Perhaps I ought to cut down the *teeniest* bit on my chalk intake," he gasped. "Do you know what I just found on *his* table? Eh? You'll never guess, never!" He waved a piece of paper in the air with his free hand. "Remember the day you magicked me? Remember that lucky day you found me in the beans? Well, he's got the words of that spell written down here, here!" He jabbed at the paper with his furry fore-finger. "He asked you for the words of that spell, didn't he?" he demanded, looking at Miss Jelly. She nodded unwillingly. The Wotsit nodded knowingly. "He knew he might need me some time in the future, so he wanted to keep a special note of the spell, just in case . . . ah, he'll miss me, I know he will . . ."

The Wotsit wiped an eye with the back of his hand.

"Never mind," he sniffed, trying to smile at the children. "Never mind. At least I saved the school for you. They won't close it now, not in a month of governors' meetings."

The children stood quiet for once and watched him.

"Now siddown!" he commanded, in his usual high bossy voice. "And your nice Miss Jelly will read the spell – and you lot gotta say it with her, see?" He sniffed again and wiped his nose with the back of his tail.

Trixie brought a milk-bottle top, Julie fetched a ruler and Miss Jelly made a wand. Rose whispered something to Miss Jelly, who nodded. Rose ran to the stock cupboard and came back with a box of assorted coloured chalk. The Wotsit's expression brightened immediately, and he wrapped his arms round the box.

"Thank you, thank you, polite little girl! Very handsome of you all, I must say, a *very* handsome present. Many thanks, one and all. But now – you'd better get on with it. . . ."

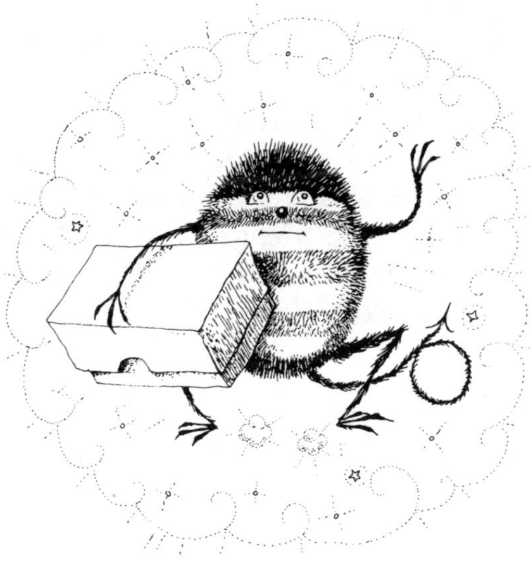

Miss Jelly cleared her throat and solemnly began to read aloud:

"Jelly – "

"*Telly*," responded the children sadly.

"Rule – "

"*School.*"

"Ale – "

"*Pale.*"

"Nosh – "

"*Posh.*"

"Gold – "

"*Old.*"

"Talk – "

"*Chalk.*"

"Thing – "

"*Bring.*"

Miss Jelly gave a half-hearted wave of her wand. There was a long silence.

"Are you really going? *Really*?" asked Rose in a small voice.

The Wotsit nodded mournfully. He was growing very pale; so was the box of chalks – pale, paler, then shimmering and transparent. He was almost invisible.

"But where are you going? Where to? Where?" asked several voices.

"Wouldn't you like to know, nosy things!" came a last high-pitched whisper. And he was gone.